# THE RUBBER STAMP ALBUM

## BY JONI K. MILLER & LOWRY THOMPSON

Designed by Louise Fili

Workman Publishing, New York

Library of Congress Cataloging in Publication Data

Miller, Joni, 1945-
Rubber stamp album.

Bibliography:p.
1. Rubber stamps. 1. Thompson, Lowry, 1954-
joint author. II. Title.
TS1920.M54     678'.34     78-7118
ISBN 0-89480-046-9
ISBN 0-89480-045-0 pbk.

© Copyright 1978 by Joni Miller and Lowry Thompson

Book Design by Louise Fili.

Jacket design by Louise Fili with special
help from Mark Huie.

Workman Publishing Company
1 West 39 Street
New York, New York 10018
Manufactured in the United States of America
First printing September 1978
10 9 8 7 6 5 4 3 2 1

We wish to thank the following for permission to include
copyrighted material:

Robert Bloomberg, assorted rubber stamp images. Copyright
1976 by Robert Bloomberg. From the All Night Media catalog.

Aaron Leventhal, assorted rubber stamp images. Copyright
1973, 1974, 1975, 1976, 1977, 1978 by Jackie Leventhal.

Jackie Leventhal, assorted rubber stamp images. Copyright
1978. From the Hero Arts catalog.

Susan Manchester, assorted rubber stamp images. Copyright
1977 by Imprints Graphic Studio. From the Graphistamp catalog.

Ronn Storro-Patterson, assorted rubber stamp images. Copyright
1978 by Nature Impressions.

We also wish to thank the following:

E.B. LaRoche, Houston Stamp & Stencil Company, Houston, Texas for photograph
appearing on page 13

Marking Device Association, Evanston, Illinois for photograph
of B.B. Hill appearing on page 10

This book was designed and produced by the
Rainbird Publishing Group.

THE RUBBER STAMP ALBUM is dedicated with appreciation beyond measure to everyone contacted during the course of its creation. Because of the warmth, excitement, energy and craziness that came our way, it was a way of life not just a book.

Walter Thompson for encouragement, ceaseless hours of errand running, advice and countless midnight favors; Jan Conner for maintaining her sense of humor while photographing some of the weirdest objects known to man; Joe Hanson for the trust and encouragement that will always give Lowry the courage to pursue her dreams; Duncan and Judi Rae for moving to Colorado — without them Joni and Lowry would never have met; Bernice (Momcat) Hall for nurturing Lowry's love of stamps; Kenny and Pumpkin Speiser for moral support, mushroom soup and, most of all, the pleasure of their company; Arthur Coons, President of Waldenbooks, for his faith and sense of humor; Molly Thompson, because she understands the importance of Dragonflies; Alison Gardner for playing kindly concierge regardless of the hour; Aunt Stephanie for walking on stamps instead of eggs; Sylvie Herold for so many kindnesses; Herb Lubalin and Ms. Bethal for introducing Louise and Lowry; Michael Krieger, Chase Caswell, Big El, Mark Huie, and David Scott for being there when the crunch came; Kendra for smiling as the fish nibbled her nose; Gene and Fran Borckardt for the dreaded Flim-Flam; Michael Tully, Lowry's mailman, who never stopped smiling no matter how crazy the delivery; Corita Kent for her graciousness; Maxine Cummings for confidence and support; David Brewbaker for providing a great source of inspiration even though he thinks he doesn't understand; Marshall, Bub and Turk for keeping Lowry awake; Gammie for Joni's typing lessons; Bob Grimes for being the happiest stamp freak we know; Estelle, Donna, Lowrie 2 and Jackie for endless hours of runarounds; Gek for his sharing; Leonore Fleischer and Barton Lidice Beneš for being from another planet; Stephen Gross for expert advise over lamp chops; Burt Stratton for proving that even a corporation like IBM could love rubber stamps; Gael Bennett for his bark; Dana Baylor for being an early supporter; E.G.G., Suzanne Freedman and geORge in geORgia for spirited correspondence.

## And

Thomas H. Brinkmann, Marking Device Association; Martin Brophy, Fulton Specialty Company (Elizabeth, New Jersey); Century Rubber Stamp Company (New York, New York); Antonio Frasconi; Ken Friedman; Gerold and Vincent; Albert W. Hachmeister, Marking Devices Publishing Company; the Institute for Advanced Studies in Contemporary Art (San Diego, California); Leavenworth Jackson; Ray Johnson; Robert Levine, Dimond-Union Stamp Works (Boston, Massachusetts); Paul M. Levy; Mark-It Rubber Stamp Company (Stamford, Connecticut); Richard Merkin; Nach and Fran; E.M. Plunkett; Schwaab, Inc. (Milwaukee, Wisconsin); Schwerdtle Stamp Company (Bridgeport, Connecticut).

# CONTENTS

THE RUBBER STAMP ALBUM
BY JONI K. MILLER & LOWRY THOMPSON

# CONTENTS

# CONTENTS  CONTENTS

# RUBBER WHAT?

**W**e used to think if one more person turned to us and said, "Rubber what?", we would start screaming and never stop. *The Rubber Stamp Album* is to answer those people, to share with them a bunch of trivia about stamps that has never been gathered together in one place before, to put stamp people in touch with each other...and most important of all, to share what we think is the greatest invention since Scotch tape ... the RUBBER STAMP.

For years stamps have been used for all manner of practical purposes: They certify that a slab of meat has been inspected and passed the test, cover up other people's mistakes, show the time of day a piece of paper crossed someone's desk, show the date a library book is due, record a bank deposit, verify a liquor shipment, confirm that a notary is really a notary, collect overdue payments (especially in times of depression), stamp trademarks on everything from bullets to lemons, open and close a border to passport bearers, price items in supermarkets and grocery stores, put markings on glass, print cardboard boxes, cancel checks, register grade markings on lumber...the list is virtually endless.

All that is one side of rubber stamps. The other more whimsical side is the one we love.

Rubber stamps have a universal and almost inexplicable appeal. The feel of a stamp in hand gives a feeling of power and command. Stamping is the grand communicator. It removes creative blocks. It makes instant art and accompanying instant gratification possible for anybody who can't draw their way out of a paper bag. In an environment that puts distance between people and things in every respect, stamps bring things into contact. When there is a sameness to things, stamps are an interrupter, a displacer, a visual pause.

They light up the mails. In post offices, silly stamped envelopes and postcards amuse and delight the people who handle them. Stamps are like opening a window for air.

Stamping has side benefits. No particular inherent artistic sophistication is required on the part of the stamper. It is completely possible to look canny and clever without actually being able to do more than give a piece of paper a good swift whack.

Stamps turn ordinary things into events. They are "anti-authoritarian in a sweet way," as George Keenen once said. They can be as anonymous as you wish, or they can expose your personal style in a singularly basic way.

We very much hope our efforts in this book will introduce you to a whole new experience, if you've never known what stamps can do. Or provide useful information you didn't have, if you're already one of the thousands stamping out life's dullness.

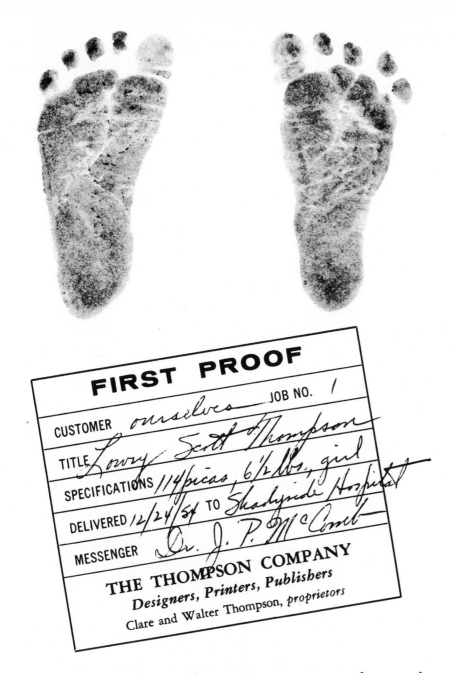

**FIRST PROOF**

CUSTOMER *ourselves*     JOB NO. *1*

TITLE *Lowry Scott Thompson*

SPECIFICATIONS *114 picas, 6½ lbs., girl*

DELIVERED *12/24/54* TO *Shadyside Hospital*

MESSENGER *Dr. J. P. McComb*

**THE THOMPSON COMPANY**
*Designers, Printers, Publishers*
Clare and Walter Thompson, *proprietors*

Most of us made a good impression at a very tender age...the good doctor pressed that tiny little foot on a stamp pad, and you made an impression for posterity minutes after bursting forth from the womb.

One thing is sure: We have yet to put a stamp in a person's hand—male, female, old, or young—and failed to see some kind of splendid activity result. We watch gleefully as children instantly swing into a physical rhythm of almost tribal intensity with two stamps and a piece of paper.

We watch grown-ups tingle and giggle and lose the question marks in their eyes.

Always remember . . . young children and white paper take good impressions.

# RUBBER STAMP HISTORY

Charles Marie de la Condamine, French scientist and explorer of the scenic Amazon River, had no idea there would ever be such a thing as a rubber stamp when he sent a sample of "India" rubber to the Institute de France in Paris in 1736.

Prior to de la Condamine, Spanish explorers had noted that certain South American Indian tribes had a light-hearted time playing ball with a substance that was sticky and bounced, but it failed to rouse their scientific curiosity.

Some tribes had found rubber handy as an adhesive when attaching feathers to their person; and the so-called "head-hunting" Antipas, who were fond of tattooing, used the soot from rubber that had been set on fire. They punctured skin with thorns and rubbed in the soot to achieve the desired cosmetic effect. The June 1918 issue of *Stamp Trade News* indicates that "rubber stamps were made hundreds of years ago. . .by South American Indians for printing on the body the patterns which they wished to tattoo," but we have been unable to verify this was actually the case. In New Zealand today, a version of such tattooing is making a hit in the form of rubber stamp "skin markers" which bear intricate figures of birds, snakes, flowers, tribal symbols etc.

It wasn't until some thirty-four years after de la Condamine sent his rubber care package home that Sir Joseph Priestley, the discoverer of oxygen, noted: "I have seen a substance excellently adapted to the purpose of wiping from paper the mark of a black lead pencil." In 1770 it was a novel idea to rub out (hence the name rubber) pencil marks with the small cubes of rubber, called "peaux de negres" by the French. Alas, the cubes were both expensive and scarce,so most folks continued to rub out their errors with bread crumbs. Rubber limped along since attempts to put the substance to practical use were thwarted by its natural tendency to become a rotten, evil-smelling mess the instant the temperature changed.

Enter Charles Goodyear. Upon hearing of the unsolvable rubber dilemma (from the Roxbury Rubber Company), Goodyear became obsessed with solving the whole sticky question once and for all. During his lifetime, Goodyear was judged to be a crackpot of epic proportions. Leaving his hardware business, he began working on the problem in his wife's kitchen, spending hours mixing up bizzarre brews of rubber and castor oil, rubber and pepper, rubber and salt, rubber and heaven knows what. Daily life intruded on his experiments in the form of recurring bankruptcy and sporadic imprisonment for failure to pay his debts. At one point, Goodyear actually sold his childrens' school books for the cash required to

embark on the next experiment. Goodyear's persistence and single-mindedness were legion.

In 1839 while fooling around in a kitchen, Goodyear accidentally dropped some rubber mixed with sulphur on top of a hot stove. Instead of turning into a gooey mess, the rubber "cured." It was still flexible the next day. The process, involving a mixture of gum elastic, sulphur, and heat was dubbed vulcanization, after Vulcan, the Roman god of fire. Vulcanized, rubber lost its susceptibility to changes in temperature. The discovery paved the way for hundreds of practical applications of rubber. In June 1844, Goodyear patented for his process. Never one to rest on his laurels, Goodyear turned his formidable energies to developing a multiplicity of uses for rubber. These continuing experiments were costly and, bless his soul, in 1860 Goodyear died two hundred thousand dollars in debt. His last words reflected the pattern of his life: "I die happy, others can get rich."

**"If you meet a man who has a rubber cap, coat, vest and shoes, carrying a rubber money purse without a cent of money in it, that will be Goodyear."**

*B.B. Hill*

## PRELUDE TO THE INVENTION OF THE RUBBER STAMP

The word "stamp," as used in historical documents, is not particularly explanatory. Neither is its cousin phrase "hand stamp." Early historical references to either can easily be mistaken for references to rubber stamps and this is not always correct. A basic assumption must be made that if the word "stamp" is used to refer to a marking device prior to 1864, it does not refer to a rubber one.

Some background on this somewhat hair-splitting problem: Metal printing-stamps, also called hand stamps or mechanical hand stamps, preceded rubber ones by six to eight years. One of the first of these was the Chamberlain Brass Wheel Ribbon Dating Stamp, which came out in the early 1860s, and another was B.B. Hill's Brass Wheel Ribbon Ticket Dater. A prolific inventor, Hill is considered to be "the father of the mechanical hand stamp." Prior to 1860, hand stamps enjoyed limited use. Their heyday commences with the Civil War. The Union financed the war by issuing revenue stamps which were required on virtually all business papers of any kind—notes, drafts, bills, checks, etc. The government required that the revenue stamps be "canceled" with a notation of the date and the name of the person canceling them. Clearly this procedure was a real pain. It was tedious and slow and begged for some type of technology to come to the rescue. It isn't difficult to imagine the instant popularity with which the first mechanical hand stamps were met.

The early days of rubber stamps and their creation are inextricably entwined with those of early dentistry. Around the same time that Goodyear received his patent on vulcanizing, anesthesia was patented by a fellow named Wells. Relatively speaking, Wells's discovery made getting your teeth pulled a moderately painless experience, so teeth were being pulled left and right. This meant, of course, that the demand for false teeth was rising proportionately. Before vulcanization, denture bases had been made primarily of gold and were both costly and difficult to make. After vulcanization, denture bases could be made of vulcanized rubber set in plaster molds. This process did not demand a great deal of skill, and soon scores of dentists had small, round vulcanizers with which to ply their trade. These were called "dental pot" vulcanizers and would be used eventually to manufacture the first rubber stamps.

## MULTIPLE CHOICE FOR THE INVENTOR OF THE RUBBER STAMP

The actual source of the first rubber stamp is still mired in mystery. It's a game of multiple choice for the inventor.

Candidate number one, L.F. Witherell of Knoxville, Illinois, caused quite a stir in June 1916, at the stamp men's convention in Chicago, by reading a paper entitled "How I Came to Discover the Rubber Stamp."

Witherell, noting that "nearly all great and marvelous inventions or discoveries have sprung into the world as a result of an accident," claimed his accidental discovery of the rubber stamp took place in Galesburg, Illinois, in 1866 while he was foreman for a manufacturer of wooden pumps. At that time virtually all identification marking was made with brass or copper stencils and paint. The pump company was experiencing problems with paint running under stencils and creating blotches on the pumps. Witherell decided to try cutting stencils out of thin sheets of rubber packing. It was while cutting letters out of a sheet of rubber, and watching the letters fall at his feet, that his brainstorm hit. He promptly cut more letters out of thicker rubber, glued them to a piece of old bedpost, inked the creation on a leather ink pad, rolled the bedpost over a pump, and made a good impression of his own initials.

*L.F. Witherell*

Unfortunately, Witherell could not whip out his bedpost stamp for an historic show-and-tell. Two years earlier, in 1914, Witherell had claimed to have the bedpost stamp still in his possession as a "potato masher," but at the convention he told the curious audience that the "sacred treasure" had been stolen from him "some years ago."

Continuing with his saga, Witherell said he next came up with the idea of vulcanized-rubber stamps and went to a dental office in Chicago where he claimed to have vulcanized "the first genuine rubber stamp in the world." Witherell's claims also extended to "the creation of the first stamp ever sold for money," which he said was made in Knoxville with the assistance of printer's apprentice O.L. Campbell, who set the type for the stamp. It was used to print on tinware.

Witherell then began to pursue his stamp career in earnest, having G.D. Colton & Co. make him a vulcanizer. He produced stamps with a series of partners, the first being B.W. Merritt, "a jolly old batchelor yankee who sold gate latches." Finally he set up his own factory with his brother and a fellow named D.A. Dudley.

Shortly after he established the factory, the Dental Rubber Syndicate demanded that Witherell pay a ten-dollars-per-pound royalty, in addition to the three-dollars-per-pound he was already paying for the flesh-colored dental rubber. Even at three dollars a pound the rubber was considered an expensive material, and Witherell found the economics of the whole thing too much to cope with. He sold the factory to Austin Wiswall of Princeton, Illinois, "who said he had

friends who could make him cheap rubber that would not infringe on the dental patents."

Witherell devoted his later years to a variety of mining enterprises and his "scientific collection of pre-historic mammals." He never relented on his numerous claims and, while in his hearty seventies, continued to remind anyone who would listen that he was still making perfect impressions with stamps he had made almost fifty years earlier . . . and that he had sold over four-thousand-dollars worth of vulcanized stamps long before anyone else made a single one.

Candidate number two is James Orton Woodruff of Auburn, New York, whose historical honors were zealously and frequently defended in stamp-trade periodicals for years by his cousin Alonzo Woodruff, who was himself to play a pivotal role in rubber-stamp history.

Perhaps as early as 1864, and no later than early 1866, James O. Woodruff visited a shop that manufactured patent washtubs where he observed the names and other identifying information being printed on the tubs with a curved wooden block which had rubber letters mounted on it. The letters had been carved from a flat piece of rubber by a man named Palmer. The lettering is said to have covered a surface four by six inches. When used with printer's ink, it left a decent, legible impression on the curved tub surfaces. While watching the tub marking, Woodruff speculated that if impressions of letters were made in vulcanizer molds, one could produce vulcanized-rubber letters.

Woodruff began playing around unsuccessfully with a vulcanizer, trying to set up a letter mold. Help was just around the corner in the person of his uncle Urial Woodruff. A dentist, Uncle Urial was very familiar with rubber, vulcanizers, and the practicalities of dealing with both. Additional experiments with a regular dental vulcanizer and Uncle Urial's advice and cooperation netted some good-quality stamps. James Orton proceeded to outfit a factory with modified versions of the dental vulcanizer, which Alonzo Woodruff described in 1908 as follows: ". . . made of boiler iron that was about 18 inches in diameter by 24 inches high, which was placed upon a stove. From the ceiling above the vulcanizer was suspended a tackle which was used to place and remove the heavy top and flasks."

With the new equipment set up, James Orton ordered in a supply of fresh, new type and prepared to set his plant in motion. The mounts for his stamps were made of black walnut in nearby Seneca Falls, New York. He personally went to pick up the first batch. Alonzo Woodruff described the outing like this: "With a bag well filled, he started up a steep hill from the shop when he soon overtook an Irish woman pushing a heavy wheelbarrow, who, with an eye to business, asked if he did not want to put his bag in the barrow and wheel it up the hill, which proposition, after some bantering, was accepted to their mutual benefit."

Woodruff, now ready for action, ran a rubber-stamp advertisement in the *Northern Christian Advocate,* a Methodist weekly published out of Auburn, New York. Orders poured in, and it looked like the first rubber-stamp killing was about to be made when disaster struck. The stamps were ruined by the only available inks. These inks contained oil as a solvent, and the action of the oil on the vulcanized rubber was calamitous. The stamps were useless, and Woodruff faced an endless line of customer complaints. Nonetheless, during this uproar, a local optimist named Rolland Dennis bought a share of the business for fifteen hundred dollars and shortly afterwards replaced Woodruff as sole owner.

Two historical artifacts of James Orton Woodruff's pioneer stamp-making days were reported to be in the care of Alonzo in 1908: one of the original black walnut mounts and "an old stool, upon the bottom of which is a

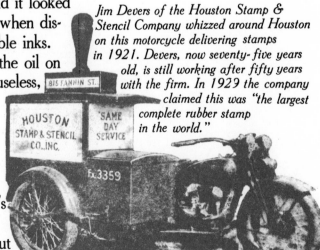

*Jim Devers of the Houston Stamp & Stencil Company whizzed around Houston on this motorcycle delivering stamps in 1921. Devers, now seventy-five years old, is still working after fifty years with the firm. In 1929 the company claimed this was "the largest complete rubber stamp in the world."*

print of one of the first rubber stamps." The impression on the stool was probably that of an American Express Company C.O.D. stamp, which had been made in Uncle Urial's dental office during the early experiments.

The least likely candidate appears to be Henry C. Leland of Lee, Massachusetts, whose cause was championed in the June 1910 issue of *Stamp Trade News* by rubber stamp manufacturer George W. Burch of Hartford, Connecticut, in an article entitled "The Invention of the Rubber Stamp." Burch had originally met Leland in Hartford in 1883. The article was the result of an interview conducted with Leland, who was then eighty-two and living in Hartford with his wife and unmarried son. The claim seems nebulous at best, but Mr. Leland has enjoyed his moment in the sun thanks to Mr. Burch's efforts. The saga:

In 1863, while on the road selling what were probably early metal-dating and cancellation hand stamps, a broom manufacturer suggested that "if he could supply a stamp that could be rolled around a broom handle to print a label, it would be a good thing."

Shortly after the suggestion, Leland moved to Pittsfield, Massachusetts, took a job in a print shop, and began toying with the idea. In his initial experiments, he set up a type form, made a plaster-of-paris cast of it, put soft rubber bands from an old printing press on the cast, set the cast on a kitchen stove, and made a primitive but successful attempt at vulcanizing with a flatiron. Encouraged, he moved to New York, took another job as a printer, and continued experimenting, this time with a dental vulcanizer. Leland worked in secret on his "invention," struggling to learn the mysteries of mold-making and the correct temperatures for vulcanizing rubber, without benefit of assistance.

Burch relates that "during the year 1864 he had got it into some shape when a near relative who lived with him and was in his confidence, gathered together what information he could . . . went to some novelty people and for a petty sum gave away all of Leland's secrets so far as he knew them. These people then came to Leland, offered to finance the patent, and induced him to accept a small sum of money for an interest in it." Leland fell for the offer, then presumably realized he'd been gulled and "in disgust threw up his claims for a patent and refused to go on with it." Shortly afterward, Leland left New York on a long trip, supporting himself by making and selling rubber initial stamps.

Who really invented the rubber stamp? As with so many inventions, the possibility exists that a number of men hit on the same idea at essentially the same time. Our vote goes to James Orton Woodruff.

SIDE VIEW

INDEXED STAMP

INDEXED STAMP Pat Dec 99

INDEXED STAMP

"The Built-in Index"

The Foundation of Successful Stamp-making

## EARLY DAYS IN THE RUBBER STAMP INDUSTRY

Rubber stamps are considered a marking device. Today Thomas H. Brinkmann, Executive Secretary of the Marking Device Association, defines marking devices as "the tools with which people . . . add marks of identification or instruction to their work or product." The earliest roots of the marking-device industry lie with early stencil makers. Many of the first rubber stamps were made by itinerant stencil makers. Since both were marking devices it was a compatible combination. The years from 1866 onward were peppered with the establishment of new stamp companies. Some were stencil makers adding stamps to their repertoire while others focused entirely on making rubber stamps.

J.F.W. Dorman is said to have been the first to actually commercialize the making of rubber stamps. He started as a sixteen-year-old traveling stencil salesman in St. Louis and opened his first business in Baltimore in 1865. In 1866 Dorman, who had enjoyed a brief career on the stage before the Civil War, learned the technique of manufacturing rubber stamps from an itinerant actor who claimed he had learned his skills from the inventor. Dorman made his first stamps under cover of night with his wife's assistance in an effort to keep the process a secret. Dorman was quite an inventor, and his contributions to the industry were numerous. His eventual specialty was the manufacture of the basic tool of the trade—the vulcanizer. His company continues in business today.

The first stamp-making outfit ever exported from the U.S. to a foreign country was shipped by R.H. Smith Manufacturing Com-

pany to Peru in 1873. Back on the home front, companies continued to spring up. In 1880 there were fewer than four hundred stamp men, but by 1892 their ranks had expanded to include at least four thousand dealers and manufacturers. An amazing number of these first companies are still in business today, frequently under their original names or merged with others whose roots lie in the mid- and late 1880s.

It was a small, tight-knit industry, characteristics it retains today. The longevity of the companies is no more astonishing than the attitude of stamp men themselves. Once in the business, people tended to stay loyal to it. During our research, we were amazed at the number of people who had spent forty or fifty or more happy years in the industry.

Early stamp makers tended to be colorful, and many frontierlike exploits dot the landscape. Louis K. Scotford and his companion Will Day set off across Indian Territory to the settlements in Texas carrying their stamp-making equipment in an old lumber wagon. The country was wild and rugged in 1876, frequented by bandits and Indians. L.K. and Will solicited orders during the day, made the stamps at night, and delivered the following day in time for the intrepid pair to harness up and head out once again. It was a romantic adventure and not unprofitable. At the end of their three thousand-mile trek, the two returned to St. Louis with two twenty-five-pound shot bags filled with silver dollars.

Charles Klinkner, who established his West Coast stamp house in 1873, would have been the pride of any modern-day publicity agent. Klinkner was prone to calling attention to his wares in startling, unorthodox ways. He rode around San Francisco and Oakland in a little red cart drawn by a donkey rakishly dyed a rainbow of colors. To make his stamps sound like something extra special, he advertised them as "Red Rubber Stamps," and people were convinced it meant something. At the time, almost all stamps were made from red-colored rubber. Ah, the power of suggestion.

After years of talk and numerous attempts to organize, the industry formed a national trade organization in 1911. M.L. Willard and Charles F. Safford, who had labored long and hard toward organizing the stamp men, saw their work bear fruit when the first marking-device trade convention took place at the LaSalle Hotel in Chicago on June 20, 1911. It was the beginning of a new era and even pioneer stamp personage B.B. Hill (the "father of the mechanical hand stamp"), then eighty years old with fifty years in the business behind him, was on hand to hear the International Stamp Trade Manufacturers Association voted into existence. Today the organization is known as the Marking Device Association and is headquartered in Evanston, Illinois.

A number of trade journals served the industry: *Stamp Manufacturer's Journal, Stamp Trade News, Marking Devices Journal,* and now *Marking Industry Magazine,* which is published under the efficient guidance of Albert Hachmeister, who acts as both publisher and editor.

*Marking Industry Magazine* is not available to individuals or companies who are not in the marking-device business, but the company does publish a useful directory each spring that anyone can order. *Marking Products and Equipment* is a complete name-and-address guide to all manufacturers and companies in the business. If you wish to receive a copy, send your request along with a check for three dollars to Marking Products and Equipment, c/o Marking Industry Magazine, 666 Lakeshore Drive, Chicago, Illinois 60611.

Since 1907, the trade publications have reflected serious industry discussions about trade ethics, price controls, planning by scientific management, and marketing, mixed with folksy anecdotes about who was playing which sport for charity and tidbits about who caught a 175-pound swordfish off the California coast. Pricing information was colorful on occasion, as witnessed by this quote from the February 1909 *Stamp Trade News:* "No blood flows from a turnip nor does wealth flow from rubber made into Rubber Stamps at 10¢ per line." The same issue proffered a real gem from a column called "Pen Points" — "Rubber stamps made while you wait' is not a good sign to hang out. It looks too easy."

**0 1 7**

# STAMP TRIVIA

## OBITUARY STAMP

One large company, unable to deal with vast quantities of mail continuing to arrive daily for an executive who had died suddenly, returned his mail to sender neatly stamped "Mr. E. Rosenblum died unexpectedly on December 4, 1976."

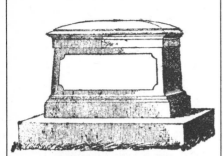

## THE POLITICAL RUBBER STAMP

Former United States Senator Chauncey M. Depew made the statement in his Fourth of July banquet speech that in the new order of politics only about 11% of the actual voters of the country constitute the government, and legislators, state and national, are rubber stamps, to carry out the will of the executive.

"The authority of the President of the United States has grown," said he, "and he now exercises more power than the czar of Russia. "But the people seem to like the change," he added, "even if it does make legislators merely rubber stamps."

*Stamp Trade News*, July 1914

## SEXIST STAMP

A West Coast realtor acknowledges his secretary's lack of typing prowess by stamping each of her poorly typed letters with SHE CAN'T TYPE, BUT SHE'S BEAUTIFUL.

## RUBBER STAMP MARRIAGE

An interesting story is told by a young Holland couple who were married by the mayor of a small fishing village, and when they reached home, they found that their marriage certificate had been stamped "CERTIFIED FOR HUMAN COMSUMPTION". Inquiry developed that the mayor also held the office of meat inspector and had used the wrong stamp.

*Marking Device Journal*, June 1932

## RUBBER STAMP DIVORCE

The papers for divorce were filed quietly last week, and the case will be heard soon—neither principal in court. It will be a quick, rubber-stamp procedure costing about $30.00, and the decree is expected to be absolute by September.

*Newsweek* magazine, May 22, 1978, on the subject of Princess Margaret's impending divorce.

## RUBBER STAMP ALIMONY

In 1964, a judge ordered an ex-husband to cease rubber-stamping the entire reverse side of his ex-wife's alimony checks because tellers were laughing at her. The stamp said THIS IS ANOTHER CHECK IN PAYMENT OF ALIMONY.

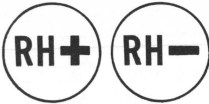

## TUMMY STAMPS??

In the 1960s, the J.P. Cooke Company in Omaha, Nebraska, created stamps with blood types on them. They were used in hospitals, especially maternity wards, and were stamped directly on the patient with edible ink. If an emergency arose, costly time was not wasted looking through files for the patient's blood type.

Cheyenne, Wyo., Feb. 1—Representative C.E. Lane wants hens to stamp their own eggs for protection of the Wyoming public. Taking a fling at house bill No. 57, which provides for the inspection, grading and labeling of eggs to show their age, he offered an amendment today in the house to require "each little red hen" to swallow rubber stamps, which would impress on her eggs information, which according to his interpretation, the bill requires.

The amendment lost, and protests that the legislature's time was being wasted followed. Majority floor leader William B. Cobb objected to what he characterized as "Mark Twain stuff," and to "jocular" amendments.

The bill was recommended for passage by the committee of the whole.

"50 Years Ago In Marking," collected from *Stamp Trade News*, February 1927, by Anne Hachmeister, *Marking Industry* magazine, Feburary 1977.

018

## RUBBER STAMP VS. HURRICANE

In 1948, "the lowly rubber stamp," the local post office, and a zealous Junior Chamber of Commerce combined forces to aid hurricane-besieged Fort Lauderdale, Florida.

It was feared that bad press in the north about the fall hurricanes and floods would damage the town's life-blood—tourism. The Chamber of Commerce ordered ten rubber stamps proclaiming the fact that FLORIDA'S TROPICAL PARADISE IS READY. THE SUN IS SHINING. A pretty young woman was stationed at a table in the post office lobby under a banner that said, "Have your mail stamped with your city's greetings," and every piece of outgoing mail reminded the public to "come on down."

## RUBBER-STAMPING THE SIDE WALKS OF PARIS

In 1912 a police decree was issued forbidding the traditional dropping of advertising handbills on the streets and sidewalks of Paris. One enterprising hawker took to wearing shoes with gigantic rubber-stamp soles. Staying within the law, he stalked the boulevards and sidewalks leaving advertising impressions in his wake. It is said he kept his ink pads damp with water from a can on his back. Water flowed through pipes concealed underneath his clothes onto the pads.

## THAT RUBBER STAMP

Woodrow has a rubber stamp;
With it signs each letter,
Causing trouble in the Camp
Woodrow
Should know
Better.

*Forbes* Magazine quoted by *Stamp Trade News*, August 1912.

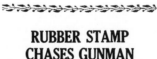

## SIMPLE SUBSTITUTE FOR STAMPS

A very simple though rough and imperfect substitute may be made by gluing with common carpenter's glue pieces of thick string upon a piece of wood, the string being given the form of the desired letters.

*Rubber Hand Stamps and the Manipulation of Rubber*, T. O'Conor Sloane, A.M., E.M., Ph.D., Norman W. Henley & Co., 1891

## RUBBER STAMP CHASES GUNMAN

When a bandit attempted to hold up Mike Zaversenuk, clerk of a Timmins hotel, the prospective victim hurled a rubber stamp at the intruder's head, whereupon the gunman turned and ran.

Quote from the Brantford *Expositor* as seen in *Marking Devices*, March 1946

## RUBBER STAMP RADIO SHOW

The Don Winslow radio program for children wove a hair-raising mystery around rubber stamps in 1938. Kellogg's sponsored the series and offered to send everyone who sent in a box top a stamp with his own initials and a design "Just like Don Winslows."

The Louis Melind Company, who made the stamps, described the plot in a bulletin: "Don has been trying to catch the spy in the naval drafting room who is plotting to steal secret naval plans. Suspecting an 'inside job,' Don decides to equip his men with some sure-fire means of identification, and works out a pocket stamp with each man's own initials worked into a naval design."

In a suspenseful climax, the hero saves the secret naval plans and his own life with his little rubber stamp.

## RUBBER STAMP ENTERTAINS ZEPPELIN PASSENGERS

Lakehurst, N.J.—Hans Hinrichs, New York business man, probably holds the Hindenburg's record for the number of postcards—somewhere around 200—sent from the airship.

He's a practical fellow. Before leaving Berlin he had a rubber stamp made.

It read: "Greetings from mid-ocean and mid-heaven."

While others were plodding away writing greetings or chewing their pens in an effort to think up something bright, Hinrichs sat there with his rubber stamp. Thud, thud, it went—and everybody laughed.

*Marking Devices*, August 1936

# HOW STAMPS ARE MADE

A few words on how stamps are made in other countries will make the typical vulcanizer method sound simple. In many parts of India they don't get beyond the mold-making stage. Rural Indians make stamp dies out of mud and use these mud stamps with the colored juices of wild flowers instead of inks. In Zambia they are making stamps out of thick animal hide. One shudders to think which animals are involved, but the impressions are said to be as fine as any made with a rubber stamp.

In principle, today's methods of stamp manufacture have changed very little from the old days of the dental-pot vulcanizer. Back then, if you wanted to test the temperature of the vulcanizer you just spat on your fingers and if the spit sizzled, the vulcanizer was ready to cure rubber. When unsure if the mold was deep enough, old-timers checked to see how the letter O looked and adjusted their compound accordingly.

Literally any piece of clear, high contrast black and white art work (preferably not a halftone) can be made into a rubber stamp.

Bob Bloomberg of All Night Media shows here how rubber stamps are made (his "rubber-stamp press" is also known as a vulcanizer).

1. A drawing is made

2. The drawing is photographed

3. The photograph is exposed onto a photosensitized metal plate. The plate is then given an acid bath which eats away at the metal, leaving a raised image of the drawing on the plate.

4. The engraved plate is placed in our rubber stamp press with a sheet of molding material and under great heat and pressure a negative mold is formed. OOOH OOWCH

5. The negative mold is placed back in the press with a sheet of rubber, producing the final positive rubber image

MEANWHILE

6. A wooden block or dowel has been cut, sanded, stamped with the image on top and then hand-rubbed with linseed oil to protect the wood. (For extremely small or large stamps, wooden molding is used.) A piece of sponge backing is cut to size and glued onto the wood and then the rubber image is cut-out and glued onto the backing.

*mountings and moldings vary between companies.

Like most other industries, the marking industry has not been left untouched by the advent of more sophisticated technology. One of the most interesting new developments involves the substitution of photopolymer resins for rubber in the manufacture of stamps. Purists will doubtless cringe over this news but it seems inevitable that the cost-saving aspects of the new method will result in a number of companies making the switch from rubber to polymer.

A growing number of patented processes exist for making polymer stamps. In words of one syllable, here is how one called Merigraph® photorelief printing plate system from Hercules Incorporated, works: A high-contrast negative transparency is placed on a photographic plate-maker that works much like an overgrown photocopying machine. The negative is covered with a very thin, clear plastic film to protect it from the liquid photo-polymer resin. Then a uniform layer of liquid polymer, along with a backing sheet, is applied on top of the protective cover film. The liquid resin is clear, slightly yellow, and has the consistency of honey. The lid of the machine is closed and sealed and the polymer and negative are exposed to ultraviolet light from top and bottom. Several minutes pass while the machine works its wonders. After exposure is completed, the plate is removed and washed in a mild detergent-and-water solution to remove unreacted resin. In the final step, the plate is put in a postexposure unit that completes the development cycle and dries it. Now the images on the plate are formed and ready to be trimmed, mounted on molding, and to emerge as stamps. Engraving, etching, matrix molding, and rubber vulcanizing are all eliminated with this process. Instead of the traditional homey red rubber, you have transparent polymer.

We've spent some time playing with stamps made with polymer and find ourselves torn between the old and the new. We like rubber; there is a realness about it. But the differences between rubber and polymer are like those between cotton and polyester —each has qualities that recommend it. Impressions made with polymer can be unbelievably fine and remarkably detailed. In most instances they are comparable to rubber, sometimes better. However, we feel that the flat areas of a polymer image simply will not take ink as well as rubber and this can result in a certain murkiness if the image contains large, raised, flat areas. The bottom line is: Polymer is fantastic for highly detailed images, not so hot for anything with a lot of plain, solid surface.

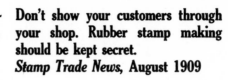

**Don't show your customers through your shop. Rubber stamp making should be kept secret.**
*Stamp Trade News*, **August 1909**

# STEP RIGHT UP, GET CHA' RUBBER STAMP CATALOG

Conventional wisdom indicates that most hardcore collectors of anything would rather turn their white-haired old mother over to the mob or give up their right arm than reveal sources of supply. Therefore it is with a mixture of pride, trepidation, and a certain heavy-heartedness that these names and addresses are being released to your care. Amassing them was a long, pleasurable treasure hunt requiring highly polished investigative skills and doglike tenacity.

Most of the companies are small, personal ones; many are owned by artists; a large percentage came into existence almost by accident. Once a rubber-stamp company or catalog starts up, the gestalt can be positively eerie. For years one company tried futilely to cease operation. It stopped sending out catalogs. It returned orders unfilled. It tried in every way possible to call a halt. But knowledge of the catalog was far-flung and it's charms notorious; and the catalog refused to die. Its founder accepted the inevitable with grace and, in a curbside meeting, gave the company away to a rubber-stamp collector whose letters he remembered liking.

As you might expect, the companies like to see those cards and letters flowing, so feel free to indulge in some fanciful correspondence when contacting them. If you think of it, bandy the name of *The Rubber Stamp Album* so they know how you got wind of them.

Pre-catalog jitters will set in once you've sent away for all the catalogs and brochures.

Dear Mr. Keenen,

Enclosed is my 50¢. I will be nervously twiddling my thumbs until your catalog arrives. You see, I work as a shipper in a book distribution warehouse, and "RELIGIOUS AND TECHNICAL MATERIALS ONLY;" "BOOKS—G DEST;" as well as: "SPECIAL HANDLING" or "AIR MAIL" stamps, they are just not getting it for me. Imagine how wonderful to see a stamped aardvark next to that "SPECIAL HANDLING" stamp. As said, I will be twitching in anticipation.

022

# YOU CALL THIS A RUBBER STAMP CATALOGUE?

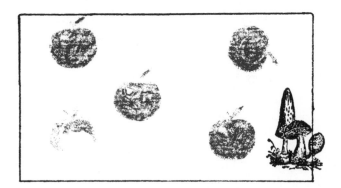

## APRIL '73

*George Keenen's first catalogue*

When the catalogs finally do arrive, there'll be an instinctive compulsion to hyperventilate and wildly order one of everything. If precautions are taken, you can order some stamps and still pay your rent. All Night Media offers this concerned medical advice in their catalog. . .

"Please take your time in looking through the catalog. When you have found the stamps you can't live without and are fumbling through your pockets for loose change or racing about the room looking for your checkbook, please pause. Pour yourself a cup of tea, find a comfortable spot and relax. We want you to receive the stamps you want, sent where you want them, as quickly as possible, and all of this requires a steady hand and a keen mind."

You see, All Night Media knows.

Use fruitfully the time spent waiting for your shipments. Stamp orders are not commonly jetted to their destinations so you'll have

several weeks in which to *really* understand your pet's problems or alphabetize your love letters.

Hardened aficionados are constantly on the prowl for stamps. Keen-eyed and diligent, they are undisturbed by dust, eager to trade stamps, and usually bear telltale ink stains under their fingernails. Vigilant to the extreme, they can be found in the following places plus some you'll want the pleasure of discovering on your own.

Many stationery stores keep a miscellaneous box of loose stamps on the shelf, and you can occasionally find an odd animal or a good sunburst buried amongst the SPECIAL DELIVERY stamps. Toy stores can be a very good source and frequently carry alphabets and animal sets. Creative Playthings stores carry their own brand of "Design Stamps" designed for children four to nine years of age. Each set has nine sanded hardwood blocks, a sheet of gray rubber shapes (a heart, a foot, a star, an egg, etc.) and a brush with six bottles of paint.

When searching in any kind of store, you should both ask if they carry rubber stamps and look for yourself. Clerks have an uncanny way of listening but not hearing and don't always understand what you have just inquired about in plain English. "Rubber what?" An important rule of thumb is that the older and crummier looking the store, the more likely it is you'll find some treats there.

Novelty and dime-stores often have good little sets for a dollar or less. Some real lulus such as a Popeye set that sat gathering dust for a year in a window display and a Manhattan Skyline set among the cosmetics have been garnered from such shops. Even grocery stores have been known to hang a novelty set or two near the creamed corn.

Regular mail-order operations such as the old and respected Lillian Vernon catalog and the slickly classy Horchow Collection sometimes show stamp sets. In 1977, Horchow had its own exclusive jungle set of seven fearsome beasts and a palm tree, which was quickly snapped up by stamp devotees. It is no longer in the catalog, but another set might appear.

Around Christmas, the seasonal novelty sets make their appearances on the scene. Generally they can be found in the same colorful mail-order catalogs that sell plastic hamburger salt-and-pepper sets. Most of these stamp sets are made in Japan, and the distinctive Japanese graphics make for some interestingly weird reindeer and Santas.

Flea markets, swap-meets, auctions, and garage sales are likely bets. Remember never, never to walk by a desk for sale without opening each drawer to see if someone left his or her stamps behind. The stamp network is replete with tall tales of people who bought big brown bags filled with forty old rubber stamps on a 105-degree day at a swap meet in Pasadena for one dollar or some equally heart-arresting price. It's rare, but it *has* been known to happen.

Old printers' cuts (often called dingbats) were made of both wood and metal and can be found at prices that vary from cheap to absurd. Most large cities have at least one store specializing in the sale of printing paraphernalia, and this usually includes cuts. Any such cut, in good enough condition, can be turned into a rubber stamp.

If the school or office you are in is an old one, it is worth taking a look to see if there are any interesting old stamps lying around.

Do not hesitate to check out the toy hordes in the possession of small acquaintances. Children often have the most amazing stamps. Be prepared to trade something substantial, as individuals twelve and under are known to drive bargains that are harder and more elaborate than those concocted by any grizzled swap-meet shark. Surreptitious raids on toy boxes is not recommended. Children have very sharp memories and the ability to carry complex inventories of everything they own in their heads.

Buy multiples whenever possible. Extras of anything good can always be used in trade with other stamp people.

There are some foreign commercial stamp companies who don't do catalogs for public consumption but sell instead to stores throughout the country.

Shachihata is a commercial Japanese stamp company whose stamps can be found in most stationery and rubber-stamp stores. Its specialty is a breed of self-inking stamp called an X-Stamper. The X-Stamper line has the usual kind of dull stock business-and-postal-phrase stamps, as well as some novelty ones. The novelty stamps look rather like giant lipsticks. They come in small, gray plastic cases with caps that snap into place to protect the stamp face. Designs include smiling and frowning faces, the soles of a pair of bare feet, seasonal greetings like MERRY CHRISTMAS, and a very Marilyn Monroe-looking lip stamp, which is pre-inked with a brilliant red ink. Now and then, it could be amusing to pucker up for the object of your affections and then attack in a blinding flash with your X-Stamper kiss!!

**ALL NIGHT MEDIA**
**Box 227**
**Forest Knolls, California 94933**

To peruse the All Night Media catalog or order a stamp from Bob Bloomberg and Marilyn Freund is likely to be one of your zanier experiences. A true renaissance duo, they make films, roller-skate backwards, and put out the silliest catalog you'll ever set eyes on. When asked to illuminate the genealogy of All Night Media, Bloomberg ran amuck with his stamps and created "The All Night Media Story" shown here.

The twenty-three-page catalog includes over 250 stamps, mostly images although there are also some pithy "editorial comment" phrases such as REPETITIOUSLY REDUNDANT and OVERRATED. Two super sets are available at somewhat lavish prices, and you might want to bear them in mind as alternatives to the standard engraved gold watch for your retirement. "Numbirds" is a thirteen-stamp set of ten raffish birds contorting themselves into numerals, plus a worm, an egg, and a feather stamp for making math symbols. "Alphabeasts" are alphabet blocks with appropriately shaped beasts representing each letter. V is a vampire, D is a dragon, and so on. Both sets come elegantly housed in handsome pine carrying-cases with sliding lids, a bottle of ink (you choose the color), and an uninked stamp pad. The bad news is "Numbirds" are $37.50, "Alphabeasts" are $75. The good news is you can buy the stamps individually (for around $3.50 each) and work your way into a set over a period of years.

All Night Media makes its own stamps with an antique stamp press that Bloomberg swears "produces sharper and cleaner images than those new fancy contraptions they got in the city." Shape and size of the image ordered determine whether yours will arrive block, dowel, molding, or handle mounted. The quality hardwood mountings are hand rubbed with "lustrous finishing oils."

The All Night Media catalog can be yours for one dollar, which is pretty cheap for a private showing of over 250 stamps, access to hard-to-find inks (like brown and orange) and the chance to chuckle frequently. Stamp prices are from $2.50 to $5. Wealthy shoppers will appreciate the directness of catalog item #252 —"All of the above, $730.75." Sigh.

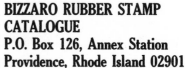

**BIZZARO RUBBER STAMP
CATALOGUE**
P.O. Box 126, Annex Station
Providence, Rhode Island 02901

Bizzaro is the most widely known of the rubber-stamp companies and has a well-earned reputation for being fun to do business with.

Multi-talented artists Kenny and Pumpkin Speiser began collecting old rubber stamps and printer's cuts for their own delight in the early 1970s. Eventually, they heaped a box with extra stamps and set them out for sale in a corner of their silk-screen studio. These first stamps were made from old zinc cuts. Pumpkin mounted the stamps herself on scraps of wood found lying around the studio. People gravitated to the box and the word began to spread. Overwhelmed at the

prospect of having to choose from so many goodies, customers soon began asking to take away impressions of the stamps so they could make cool-headed decisions in the privacy of their own homes. Pumpkin began stamping out huge poster-catalogs, and

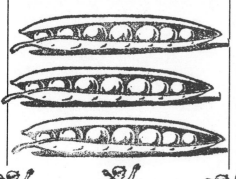

the Bizzaro Rubber Stamp Catalogue was on its way.

Now the catalog is an enticing fifteen-page adventure filled with more than three-hundred-and-fifty temptingly eclectic stamps of clowns, fedoras, slices of pie, trolls, luxury liners, palm trees, car crashes and a stately tombstone. The stamps, which sell for around $2.50 each, are mounted on light-colored wooden moldings.

It's often difficult to find certain inks and pads so public-service-minded Bizzaro thoughtfully offers two sizes of Carter's® Micropore® stamp pads (in a choice of five colors) as well as special food inks and un-inked foam stamp pads. The food inks are U.S. Government approved vegetable dyes, 100 percent edible and water soluable. Bizzaro Food Stamps (Homemade, Fresh, etc.) are handy when used with edible ink to leave your mark in unnatural ways on food.

One dollar will get the Bizzaro Rubber Stamp Catalogue into your clutches and your name on the mailing list for coming attractions.

**CLEARSTAMP**™
**20 Waterside Plaza, #25F**
**New York, New York 10010**

"Clearstamps™" are a sterling example of that old saw Necessity is the mother of invention. For years Ernest Burden, an architectural delineator, painstakingly drew trees, people, cars and aerial views of foliage on his architectural renderings while plagued with the thought— there must be an easier way. Stamps were clearly the answer, but rubber ones didn't fit the bill. Exact, precise positioning is essential in rendering, and the stamps had to allow an architect to see exactly where he was stamping. In 1967, Burden hit on the "Clearstamp™" concept. He started taking hundreds of photographs of trees, rocks, cars, and people typically used in rendering. The most suitable photos were submitted to a select group of fellow architects to determine usability and appropriateness. Then the photos were converted into the first "Clearstamps™."

The stamps are totally transparent! You can see right through them. Each design is impressed on a clear vinyl printing surface which is bonded to a polished lucite block. You can't fail to get a buzz off "Clearstamps™" purely as physical objects—their clean lines and ethereal presence are simply boggling. They could easily be sculptures from Mars. So satisfying are they just to look at, it would be criminal to keep them stored away when not in use.

The wearing qualities of vinyl are long-

term. More importantly, "Clearstamps™" make unusually fine and delicately precise impressions. The detailing on the foliage stamps is incredible. Although any rubber-stamp ink and pad can be used, best results are obtained with a Carter's® Micropore® pad. Cleaning is easy: Gently wipe with a cloth saturated in denatured alcohol or run warm water over the printing surface immediately after use. Vinyl characteristically yellows with age, so don't panic if, after a few months of use, your "Clearstamps™" show signs of incipient jaundice.

"Clearstamps™" come in three varieties—individual stamps, "Clearcubes" and "Supercubes." "Clearcubes" are a good deal since you get four same-size designs mounted on one cube of polished lucite with two surfaces left free for gripping. You can save approximately twenty percent on a "Clearcube" versus the cost of four separate stamps. "Supercubes," a specialty item, have two designs in three sizes mounted on a very large cube.

The twelve-page "Clearstamp™" catalog is free on request. If you'd like a small sample "Clearstamp™," mention *The Rubber Stamp Album* when you write, and the Burdens will send you one *free*. Prices range from $2.50 to $15.

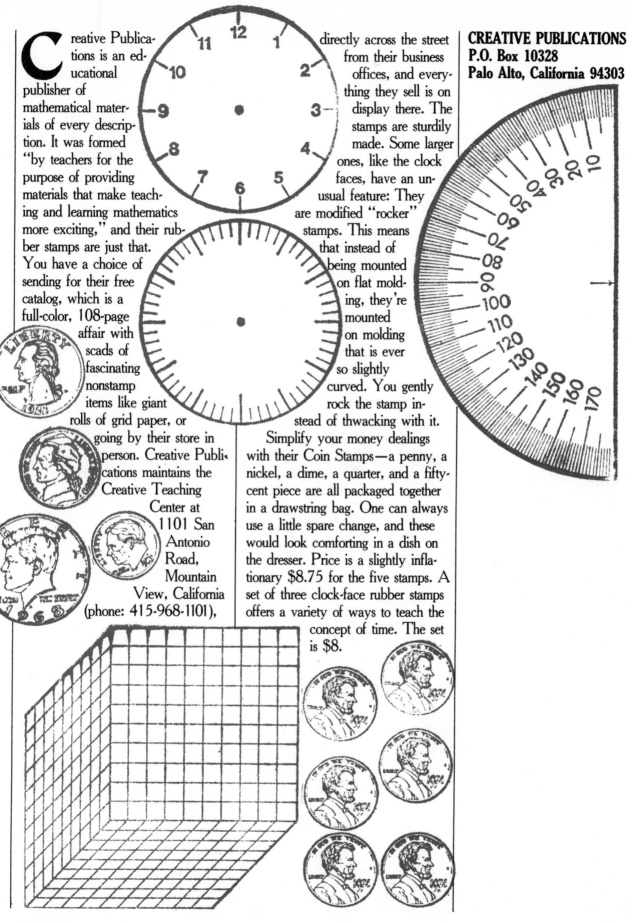

Creative Publications is an educational publisher of mathematical materials of every description. It was formed "by teachers for the purpose of providing materials that make teaching and learning mathematics more exciting," and their rubber stamps are just that. You have a choice of sending for their free catalog, which is a full-color, 108-page affair with scads of fascinating nonstamp items like giant rolls of grid paper, or going by their store in person. Creative Publications maintains the Creative Teaching Center at 1101 San Antonio Road, Mountain View, California (phone: 415-968-1101),

directly across the street from their business offices, and everything they sell is on display there. The stamps are sturdily made. Some larger ones, like the clock faces, have an unusual feature: They are modified "rocker" stamps. This means that instead of being mounted on flat molding, they're mounted on molding that is ever so slightly curved. You gently rock the stamp instead of thwacking with it.

Simplify your money dealings with their Coin Stamps—a penny, a nickel, a dime, a quarter, and a fifty-cent piece are all packaged together in a drawstring bag. One can always use a little spare change, and these would look comforting in a dish on the dresser. Price is a slightly inflationary $8.75 for the five stamps. A set of three clock-face rubber stamps offers a variety of ways to teach the concept of time. The set is $8.

**CREATIVE PUBLICATIONS**
**P.O. Box 10328**
**Palo Alto, California 94303**

**DOUGLAS HOMS
CORPORATION
1538 Industrial Way
Belmont, California 94002**

Twenty years ago, canny commercial-stamp mogul Douglas Homs worked out the assiduously practical "Dial-A-Phrase" idea. Each of his five stamps provides twelve words or phrases in one. The phrases are listed on a metal cover and each has a number. You simply select the number of the phrase you wish to use, turn a selector key mounted on the side to the corresponding number, and you've got it. The actual stamp portion is a seamless rubber belt that revolves inside the cover. Three of the stamps are most suited to use by businesses or rabid letterwriters as they contain postal instructions. The fourth is a friendly money-collection device — one that provides eleven somewhat civilized, gentle requests for payment and one dreaded final-notice phrase. The real corker is the Homs

Teacher's Stamp. Not only will "pupils respond to these attention-getting appraisals of their work," but corporate memos might profit from their light-hearted graphics. Several phrases would be especially handy for commenting on gross margin, and the merit ribbon that says "excellent" could be experimented with as a substitute for bonuses. Well, perhaps *that* isn't feasible, but certainly you don't have to be a teacher to appreciate the instant communication this big stamp offers. The Teacher's Grading Stamp is $11.95 (this makes each phrase cost a little under $1.), and the others range from $2.95 to $11.95. The stamps can be found in stationery and business supply stores, or write directly to Douglas Homs Corporation and request their free brochure on "Dial-A-Phrase" stamps.

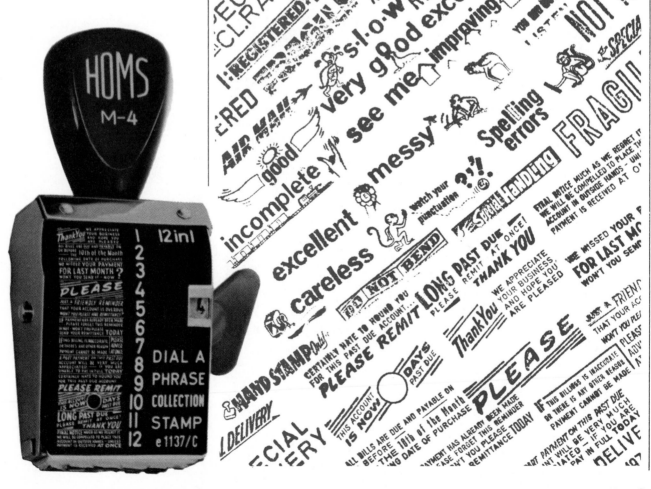

The Flim-Flam catalog will absolutely make your heart stop. It is a fifty-six-page groaning board of over fourteen hundred stamps. Months are required to fully absorb its contents.

Gene Borckardt claims to be the "biggest rubber-stamp maker in America," for reasons that have nothing whatsoever to do with his stamp production. He's a whopping 6'5", 240 pounds of good cheer. A linotype repairman by profession, he has collected printer's paraphernalia for over twenty years. Some years ago his collecting mania led to the purchase of the contents of an entire old print shop that was going out of business. He bought the whole thing, including several thousand printer's cuts which were added to his already

extensive collections. Circumstances forced the Borckardts to start selling off the cuts. The experience was too heartbreaking, so Gene and his wife Fran came up with the idea of making rubber stamps from the cuts and selling them instead. Flim-Flam set up shop at the Aurora Farms Swap Meet in 1970. Figuring that most

people assume they'll get flim-flammed at a swap meet, they named themselves accordingly.

Their swap-meet days are now passed, and now Flim-Flam is strictly mail-order. Gene makes his own stamps, right down to the wooden molding. Sometimes the stamps are handle mounted, sometimes molding mounted, depending on the design ordered. Prices are remarkably reasonable, starting at $0.50 and working their way upward. The range of designs is awesome so the $2 for the catalog is really a bargain.

A Flim-Flam stamp will enhance anything under the sun. There's a stamp of a postman delivering mail that is good to know about when Christmas rolls around

and you're at a loss about what to give that patient mailman. If it's food you're addicted to, Flim-Flam can sell you bread and jam or hamburgers or cake or a dozen eggs. A series of Art Nouveau-style flowers will help make stationery in seconds. You'll never be the same after the Flim-Flam catalog.

**THE FLIM-FLAM SHOP**
17800 Chillicothe Road
Unit 110
Chagrin Falls, Ohio 44022

**GRAPHISTAMP™**
**IMPRINTS GRAPHIC STUDIO**
**Box 2868**
**Carmel-by-the-Sea, California 93921**

Susan Manchester, an etcher and wood block printer who studied in Florence, started making stamps several years ago after finding her child's dime-store stamp sets fun, but not quite fun enough. Her first stamp design went into immediate use on her business card and was followed by a series of personalized stamp designs created for her favorite children. Friends prodded Susan and partner David Smith, a residential architect, to start a stamp business, and Graphistamp™ was formed as an adjunct to their graphic design studio. The studio, by the way, incorporates rubber stamps in its assignments at the drop of a hat.

Graphistamp™ designs are delicately formal, self-contained, and very slick. There are over thirty individual stamp designs to choose from, plus a terrific Celtic, illuminated alphabet. Your initial from the alphabet is just the thing to tuck away for a rainy day. You can spend a monstrous amount of time contentedly illuminating one with colored felt-tip pens. Tends to bring out the monk in most people.
The stamps have

a fine rubber relief printing surface and a sort of odd, chunky T-shaped solid hardwood handle. Some very useful stamps say things like FROM THE GARDEN OF and FROM THE WINE CELLAR OF along with an appropriate design. Susan's feather stamp is very special when combined with some real feathers on an envelope. A Graphistamp™ with the deluxe fancy packaging in a box includes a small stamp pad and a very nicely put together brochure illustrating Graphistamp™ at work on invitations, labels, parcels, and pictograms. The deluxe packaged deal is $8—or you can order no frills, just a stamp by itself for $6. Send $1 and Susan will send a big brochure with all the stamps shown. She'll even accept credit-card orders.

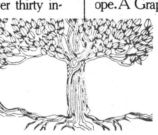

**EX LIBRIS**

**from the GARDEN of**

032

**HERO ARTS**
P.O. Box 5234
Berkeley, California 94703

Hero Arts takes its name from a gentle feminist children's story about a girl named Hero who, after overcoming the dreaded candy-bandit and saving Prince Alarming, refuses to marry and opts instead for a life of adventure on the high seas. The illustrations in the book (no longer particularly characteristic of her work) are all rubber stamps designed by Jackie Leventhal, who used to be a widely-known Bay Area photog-

rapher before her transformation into "The Rubber Stamp Lady." For the past several years, her name has been virtually synonymous with rubber stamps on the West Coast.

In 1974, Jackie received a rubber-stamped letter from photographer Ellen Brooks, and was so "buzzed out" by it that she immediately took a drawing of her own hand, and one of Batman by son Aaron, to the nearest commercial stamp-maker to have them converted into stamps. A short time later, she borrowed a discarded vulcanizer from a high-school graphic arts department and began making stamps for her own use. Eventually she started taking the stamps to craft fairs, where she spent hours perched at a table with a rainbow assortment of colored marking pens hand-coloring the stamps to show their versatility. Jackie notes that

in the early days there wasn't much familiarity with stamps, and tastes ran to butterflies. Now tastes are more sophisticated, the graphic leanings more bizarre. Her $1 catalog reflects the changing tides. Butterflies and ballerina frogs share catalog honors with a stamp of a feline seductress singing a tune into an old mike, and a lively cartoon alphabet. Many of the newer designs are the inspired fancies of San Francisco animator, Sally Cruikshank. The stamps, completely handcrafted in Jackie's own workshop, are beautifully mounted on blocks of fine, select woods, and each block bears the impression of the stamp on top of the mount for easy identification. Special orders are welcomed and usually cost between $10 and $25. Stamps seen in the catalog are from $3.25 to

$4.75. If the choice is too hard to make and you want to give the stamps as a gift, Hero Arts offers amusing gift certificates.

Unfortunately, Jackie no longer holds group classes in stamp making as she once did (Jessica Katzen, who is Rubberstampede, was an early student); but if your interest is serious, and Jackie has the time, arrangements can be made for private sessions. Her son, Aaron, is active in rubber-stamp circles and his contributions to the art can be seen further on, in the section about the International Rubber Stamp Art Exhibitions.

**MARY ALICE SCENIC STAMPS™**
2453 Echo Park Avenue
Los Angeles, California 90026

boyboyboyboyboy

**D**uring the wild and woolly sixties in California, Mary Alice wandered into a junk shop one day and spied an old rubber-stamp sign-marker set, complete with its original wooden box, lying dust-covered in a corner. The price was reasonable, but more than Mary Alice could afford at the time. For weeks she thought about the stamps. Eventually, she went back to the shop, made a deal with the owner and returned each week for months to plunk down a miniscule weekly payment. That alphabet got quite a work out through the years making "Welcome Home" signs to greet a grandmother returning from adventures in India, banners for weddings held on the beach and a wide array of silly signs.

Now Mary Alice is selling the same kind of wonderfully handy rubber-stamp alphabets (alas, not in wooden boxes) in a variety of serif and sans-serif styles. Each alphabet comes boxed with a stamp pad; some come with both upper and lower case letters as well as numerals, complete punctuation and a pointing hand. One set is an elaborate Old English set ideal for stamping out official looking proclamations. The alphabets run between $15 and $20.

The gem in the catalog is a nostalgic looking picture and word set— twenty-eight picture stamps and fifty-nine words—just like the sets children used long ago to make their own stories. It's reasonably priced at around $25.

Mary Alice's catalog is $1 and includes other stamps in addition to the alphabets. There's a clock-face without hands (about $2.75), a set of U.S. coins of the realm (around $5), a set of eight basic geometric shapes (about $9) and a useful set of holiday stamps (rabbit, pumpkin, Abe Lincoln, etc.) for annotating your calendar that is around $3.50, plus a selection of individual designs.

Mary Alice is also purveyor of a special series of educational stamps. Blissymbolics© is a "visual, meaning-based communication system" used internationally for teaching the handicapped or nonspeaking person to communicate effectively. Each symbol stamp also shows the word equivalent to enable others to follow and understand.

_____ o'clock

A a  An an am bear bird bread boy bee big cat Can chicks cow can duck donkey dog fox fish goose goat girl hen horse Has has Have have How how is it I little mouse My my owl play pig rooster rabbit sheep run See see squirrel to turkey The the wolf You you wheat This That . , ! ?

034

**M**inkey, "The Wrestling Stamp King," has been making stamps since 1968, when he decided to combine his love of wrestling with an urge to make stamps.

His early profits were used to put his daughter Patty through wrestling school and support her while she turned into a professional wrestler known as Patty Stevens, "White Venus." In a unique burst of fatherly devotion, Minkey has immortalized Patty as one of his twenty-two rubber stamps. His other stamps depict various wrestling activities as well as halftone photographic portraits of well-known professional wrestlers.

The current selection of stamps is shown on a brochure you can get by sending Minkey a stamped, self-addressed envelope and $0.25. Each stamp is around $2.75, or you can go whole hog and take advantage of his liberal special deal—ten stamps of your choice for $10.

**MINKEY'S RUBBER STAMPS**
2563 West Barton Square
Fresno, California 93725

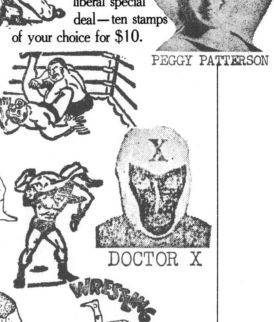

PEGGY PATTERSON

DOCTOR X

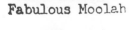
Fabulous Moolah

MR. WRESTLING

CHIEF JAY STRONGBOW

0 3 5

**NATURE IMPRESSIONS®**
**99 Ardmore Road**
**Kensington, California 94707**

Ronn Storro-Patterson, a biologist with a whale habit, caught stamp fever after reading an article about rubber stamps in a local newspaper. The article prompted him to have a whale stamp made to use on his personal correspondence. So many people who saw the stamp wanted to buy one that Ronn launched Nature Impressions® by offering a selection of eight whale stamps designed to "promote and aid whale consciousness." Sales of the stamps make it possible for Ronn to actively pursue his devotion to the study and protection of whales.

The stamps cost around $4 each and are mounted on a block of eastern beech molding with an impression of the design on top of the molding for easy identification.

His selection is expanding rapidly and he has a vision of using stamps to promote "good public relations for unpopular animals" of all kinds. His $0.50 brochure shows a variety of stamps arranged in "sets"—desert animals, seashore life, mountain animals, marine mammals, owls, etc. Each series of stamps is designed to "illustrate the bio-geographic diversity of the United States."

Teachers should note that these stamps are handy, accurate teaching aids.

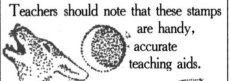

In 1893, at the tender age of twenty-four, J.M. Patrick established one of the first West Coast stamp houses with a modest initial stock worth less than five hundred dollars. J.M. was one of the most active of the pioneer stamp men, and to this day the company remains a family business headed by his equally involved son, Howard. Through the years, the thrust of the business turned toward printing and stationery items. Then, in the early 1960s, a fateful phone call signaled the beginning of a new era. A customer wanted to know if Patrick's could provide a rubber stamp of an airplane. A brief search of the Patrick plant turned up an old cut of one and the stamp was made and sent over to the store.

The customer never showed up for the stamp, and employee Bob Grimes, who has spent more than twenty-five years behind the counter

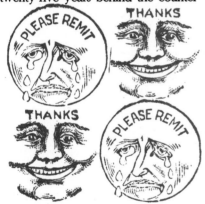

at Patrick's, began playing with it. The stamp quickly became an obsession, and Grimes found himself sending tons of air-mail letters as an excuse to fool with the stamp. Recipients of the letters were charmed, and Grimes had a supply of the planes made up to sell. They were an instant hit, and to broaden the selection he began dipping into boxes of old cuts stored in a corner of the plant.

The unusual delights at Patrick's spread by word of mouth through the Bay Area. Now literally thousands of stamps are kept in bins in the store. It is worth a trip to San Francisco just to sort through them in person. You name it, and Patrick's has a stamp of it—from pointing hands and flies to strawberries and cable cars.

Grimes himself is an integral and much loved part of Patrick's charm. His infectious devotion to stamp madness can convert the most hardened curmudgeon into a stamping fool. A few months ago, a woman stopped right in the middle of her frenzied stamping, walked over to Grimes, looked up, and admonished him, "Don't ever grow up." For Grimes it was "the nicest thing a customer ever said to me. I don't think I could if I tried."

Grimes likes to keep a small supply of loose stamps at the front counter near some paper and pads, for customers to play with as they wait, and notes that few are able to wrench themselves away in a reasonable length of time.

The 10-page catalog is free and shows more than 150 stamps, including the airplane that started it all, at prices ranging from $1 to $4.

**PATRICK & CO.**
**560 Market Street**
**San Francisco, California 94104**

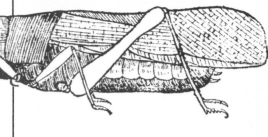

Slowly, with great feeling.

If a bod-y trust a bod-y

And fail to get prompt pay,

May a bod-y ask a bod-y

Please re-mit to - day?

**READANCE RUBBER STAMP SERVICE**
10617 Linnet Avenue
Cleveland, Ohio 44111

The early days of this commercial rubber-stamp company were harrowing. It was a "closet" operation set up without the landlord's knowledge in the Readance's apartment. Forewarned of landlord visits, the Readances would hide their stamp-making equipment in the bedroom. Surprise visits were dealt with by throwing fabric and dress patterns over the offending equipment in the hope that the landlord would think Mrs. Readance was in the throes of a sewing spree.

Readance offers a unique, personalized, pet-breed rubber-stamp service for name-and-address stamps. The choice of animals is awesome—120 dog breeds, 20 horse breeds, 20 cat breeds, plus a miscellany category that includes a fish, a rabbit, a

turkey, a parakeet, a hippo, and a lion's head. The dogs are thoughtfully broken down by categories: sporting dogs, hounds, terriers, nonsporting, and working dogs. This could be your long-awaited chance to satisfy a yearning for a Bedlington Terrier or a Japanese Spaniel. For around $5.98 you can have the pet of your choice perched above your name and address.

Mr. Mrs. John Packard
3583 Lakeview Dr.
Riverside, Calif. 94521

Have a nice day

Have a nice day

Readance also has some rather corny but cheery Christmas designs intended for combining with your name and address for stamping merry yuletide correspondence and packages. These, too, are around $5.98.

The ubiquitous smiling-face design that you can't escape from is available with several different phrases for $2.25. Readance will even whip up a name-and-address stamp in your own handwriting for $7.95. All stamps come sturdily made with wooden handles for a lifetime of use. Well, almost a lifetime. There was the woman who ordered a stamp with her dog on it only to call with a reorder ten days after she received it. Her dog had chewed up the stamp! Readance will send a free brochure with ordering information upon request.

Sandra Olsen
Box 121 A
Gosport, IN. 47433

Joyce C. Murphy
P.O. Box 372
Cocoa Beach, FL. 32931

Mrs. Raymond R. Sinotte

Carolyn A. Steinla

Mr. Keith D. August

Red Rubber Valley came into existence several years ago for the straightforward capitalistic purpose of making money. Its founders, Marie Dern and Martha Shaw, set the tone of the catalog by appearing on its cover stylishly garbed in Red Cross nurses' uniforms.

Most of Red Rubber Valley's images are original, many by artist Richard Shaw who has the kind of offbeat visual sense that gives birth to things like a stamp of a pot on a stove with

rising steam spelling out *Thanks*.

Two of the most intricate stamps are actually tattoo designs by San Francisco tattoo artist Don Hardy.

A selection of very small stamps is sold as "variety sets" and are modestly priced considering the number of stamps involved—usually eighteen per $10 set.

There are super alphabets including a large one on blocks of wood, which is perfect for small hands, and a bizarre animal ABC.

Martha and Marie love making stamps out of kids' drawings. If you send a copy of the masterpiece you wish transformed into a stamp, they'll send you back an estimate. Of course, they don't discriminate and will do custom work for grown-ups' designs too.

The most irresistible offering from Red Rubber is rebus sets. They are out of this world. Time out for a rebus definition from the American Heritage Dictionary: "A riddle composed of words or syllables depicted by symbols or pictures that suggest the sound of the words or syllables they represent."

There are two rebus sets, each containing over twenty stamps, which were issued originally, under the name Tuxedo Brand & Co., as signed, limited-edition art events. The present re-issues come in handmade boxes covered with gorgeous "French marble paper" just like the originals. Unsigned sets are $40; sets signed by the artist are $50. The designs are all by Richard Shaw, founding member of Tuxedo Brand, a band that delights in getting spiffed up in tuxes to play hillbilly music.

Stamp prices run the gamut from $3 for an individual stamp to $50 for signed sets. Red Rubber Valley once ran an ad stating it would send anyone its free catalog for a buck, but the real truth is it will send you the dollar catalog for a dollar.

**RED RUBBER VALLEY**
**P.O. Box 127**
**Fairfax, California 94930**

039

**ROLLERWALL™, INC.**
**P.O. Box 757**
**Silver Spring, Maryland 20901**

Rollerwall is a version of an old European design-painting technique which utilizes design rollers. Think back on the hallway walls of buildings put up in the 1930s and 1940s. Remember the way it looked as if they had been wallpapered, but when you got closer you could tell the design was painted on? It looked like stenciling, and the patterns were generally very geometric, Deco-style ones. This is the technique used.

Two bits of paraphernalia are required—an applicator (around $8) and a design roller made of a rubber substance (around $7). A Feeder roller, made out of a spongy material, snaps into a metal frame which is mounted on a wooden handle. The design roller is a kind of tubular rubber stamp, and it fits against the feeder.

Use flat oil-base or flat latex paint. Dip the feeder in the paint and start rolling on the wall, just as if you were using a regular paint roller, and designs will magically appear on the wall before you can say "rubber."

There are over a hundred design rollers to choose from—some are very forties-looking in charming ways, others not. There are designs with ducks and horses and hearts and roses and, incredibly, one with a wood-grain pattern.

The rollers can be used on any flat surface, from walls and paper to old furniture. People involved with set design, especially for low-budget amateur theater, will find Rollerwall™ handy. "Last year I used one of your rollers to paint the stage for my production of *Arsenic and Old Lace*. The effect was stunning." This is an observation found in the free brochure, which will be sent upon request to those interested.

Marilyn Housley found herself involved with stamps quite by accident. For years she and her husband have collected antique printer's cuts. One day someone suggested she try stamping on paper with them. The resulting impressions were poor, but the experience prompted Marilyn to start making rubber stamps from the cuts; and the Rubber Stamp Catalog made its debut in 1976. Since then she has shipped stamps around the world to customers who run the gamut from servicemen and doctors to prisoners and ministers.

One customer named Weiner makes his mark with the Rubber Stamp Catalog's sausage stamp, while another, in prison, uses his stamps to create greeting cards which he sells to fellow inmates.

Marilyn, whose background lies in design, notes that "word-of-mouth is important" in spreading the word about her catalog. One prospective customer who had seen the catalog at a friend's house, sent her catalog request in a fingerprint covered envelope pleading "You must send me a catalog because my fingers are wearing out."

The twelve-page catalog is one dollar and shows over two hundred and fifty designs plus an alphabet. Catalog highlights include a tiny laughing bear, a juicy looking bunch of grapes and a smiling telephone equipped with arms and legs. All stamps are molding mounted. Prices range between $2 for very small stamps to $4 for larger ones.

**THE RUBBER STAMP CATALOG**
**P.O. Box 209**
**Bristol, Rhode Island 02809**

**RUBBERSTAMPEDE**
1572 Euclid Avenue
Berkeley, California 94708
Phone: 415-841-1878

A used vulcanizer at a good price is the dream of every true stamp nut. When Jessica Katzen ran across a good deal on one in early 1977, it took her a good swift three seconds to figure out the only way she could afford to own it was to become a rubber-stamp company. Jessica bought the vulcanizer and became Rubberstampede, a concern devoted to supporting her personal stamp habit as well as supplying others with "rubber stamps...that can keep your child, grown-up or unwanted houseguests occupied for hours of quiet play."

Jessica has been involved with stamps for ages and fondly remembers the cliched simplicity of one of her first stamps, which was created in cahoots with her high-school beau. It read *Sincere good wishes to a dear friend,* and this intimate sentiment was stamped with abandon on numerous high-school yearbooks.

People are prone to drop by Jessica's house to make their purchases, and she gets a kick out of watching them become obsessive under her watchful gaze. It is the same old story...give someone a few stamps and some blank paper and... well, you know.

Rubberstampede has some great designs. A series of quilt-pattern stamps has a zillion uses; and the German trade symbols, circa 1907, have bold, clear graphics and would make

perfect presents for anyone whose trade matches. The bird images are marvelous, especially the duck.

The Rubberstampede catalog is a repository of more than 150 stamps, costs $1 and is accompanied by an outpouring of friendly advice on using stamps. A glutton for communication, Jessica welcomes phone calls from those "needing emergency relief or who want to gossip about whose uncle was seen surreptitiously using a rubber stamp in the 3rd floor bathroom."

A few years ago Doris Chelmow wracked her brain in search of an unusual gift for a cat lover and came up with the idea of a cat's-paw rubber stamp. She had one custom made, and the friend was "purrfectly" delighted. Doris pondered her friend's reaction and swiftly brought out her first stamps under the company name Lipsack and Catsack.

That cat's-paw has seen a lot of action since, making appearances in a variety of mail-order catalogs and a host of stores throughout the country.

Artist Remy Charlip used it in his work "Poor Polly," which shows the paw making its way across the paper leaving colorful stray feathers in its wake.

Gripped by stamp madness, Doris has continued with other practical designs—a dog's paw in response to demands for equal time from certain pet lovers, a green thumb, a shooting star for actor friends, a kosher seal of approval, and a pair of deliciously kissey lips (if pushed on this one, Doris *will* admit...).

The stamps, which are handle mounted, are available two ways. For $3 postpaid you get a stamp, plain and simple. For $5.50 postpaid, the stamp comes cleverly packaged in a little drawstring muslin sack accompanied by a small stamp pad of an appropriate ink color —purple with the kosher stamp, brown with the dog's paw, screaming ruby red with the lips.

A brochure showing a variety of stamps is available free.

**17TH STREET RUBBER WORKS**
110 East 17th Street, Apt. 2F
New York, New York 10003

IT'S KOSHER כשר

IT'S KOSHER כשר

WITH LOVE

043

**SQUIRE & SMALL**
**178 Fifth Avenue**
**New York, New York 10010**

No one has had the courage to ask Neil Small what libidinal need prompted him to make a kiss stamp in 1972 (or even to inquire whose kiss it really was), but he surely had subway posters in mind as a stamping ground for his instant graffiti handlebar-moustache stamp. If you are contemplating growing a moustache, he suggests you get a preview by stamping a photo of yourself before actually taking the plunge.

Squire & Small stamps come packaged in a sturdy "gift box" with a small ink pad and a card showing suggested uses. Since this company puts out a line of slick-looking gift items, you'll find information on its stamps combined with other things in a free brochure available upon request. Each stamp is $5.50 postpaid. Information on its stamps combined with other things in a free brochure available upon request. Each stamp is $5.50 postpaid. Other Squire & Small designs include an early sixteenth-century sunburst that is very striking and a pleasantly baroque angel/cherub/cupid.

This unusual company was discovered while on a sick leave spent gracefully reclining in a big brass bed sipping curative beverages and weakly fingering a pile of old needlecraft magazines.

Each Stamp'N Stitch™ kit contains a vial of washable ink, a small dry ink pad, a plastic handle, and a sheet of gray rubber images. You gently tear the perforated pieces of rubber apart to separate the stamps, then mount them temporarily as needed on the plastic handle. The idea, a clever one, is to use the rubber stamps to mark embroidery designs on fabric instead of using the usual tissue embroidery transfers. After you have stitched over the designs, wash the fabric and they'll disappear, leaving your unsullied stitching behind. Each kit is $4.95 postpaid and you get to choose *one* set of rubber designs—a large cross-stitch alphabet or a small cross-stitch alphabet, animals, flowers, or border designs.

If you wish to purchase only the rubber sheets of designs, they are $1 per set. Replacement plastic handles cost the same. The designs are large and simple, making them especially appealing to children. Try

mounting the pieces of rubber yourself on scraps of wooden molding for some great cheap stamps.

This company also manufactures an indelible marking kit that includes a set of small, unmounted rubber letters. These are usually used for marking the clothing, etc., of children

on their way to camp. Send a stamped (with postage, that is), self-addressed envelope when requesting the free brochures and ordering information.

STAMP'N STITCH™
75R Chamberlain Avenue
Elmwood Park, New Jersey 07407

**STRAW INTO GOLD**
5533 College Avenue
Oakland, California 94618

Straw Into Gold is actually a shop and mail-order catalog devoted to supplying spinners and dyers with a myriad of hard-to-get items. In its infinite wisdom, the shop has assumed its customers would enjoy stamping everything in sight with sheep and offers a fanciful assortment of eight sheep stamps. Each stamp is approximately $3, and new sheep are added to the flock regularly. If you contribute a new design to the cause and it's used, Straw Into Gold will send you a free stamp. Hooray for the spirit of barter!

Also included in the catalog is a section devoted to describing feathers sold by the half ounce, which have interesting possibilities as envelope decorations. A mere $0.50 will obtain the forty-five-page catalog.

**VICTOR GRAPHICS**
1330 Arrow Highway
P.O. Box 538
La Verne, California 91750

If you're in the midst of an identity crisis or poised on the brink of fame and notoriety, an autograph stamp is a useful thing to have tucked away. It's a perfectly acceptable way to make your mark. Even the Russian government allowed illiterate peasants in the 1920s to leave their mark on official documents with a rubber-stamped signature. Victor Graphics will zip out your signature as a handsome, photopolymer stamp with a quality wooden molding mount for a very reasonable $2.25 postpaid. Just write your signature clearly in black ink on a white piece of paper, tell them you want it converted to a stamp, enclose a check or money order, and in a week or two the tedium of dealing with autograph hounds is solved.

Originally autograph or signature stamps were made by writing the signature with ink on paper and transferring the writing by moistening the paper and pressing it to a block of wood. The wooden block was then carved with the signature and used to make a rubber-stamp mold.

Remember when ordering that nothing says it has to be your actual signature. If deep under the skin you always knew you were Attila the Hun, there is nothing that says you can't fake it.

046

**YOU CALL THIS A RUBBER STAMP CATALOGUE?**
**Eileen Hitsky**
**904 Panoramic Way**
**Berkeley, California 94704**

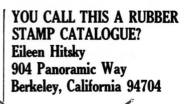

During the early seventies, this catalog's originator, George Keenen, otherwise known as Gek, spent pleasant times playing around with his rubber stamps, some of the first of their kind seen in California, and just sort of mildly letting people in on a new world of visual lunacy. Then, as now, rubber stamps were "to big art as a pin is to a balloon" and early Keenen stamps found their way quite literally around

the world. They were recorded for posterity in Hervé Fischer's book, *Art et Communication Marginale: Tampons d'Artistes;* and in that good old counter-cultural artifact, *The Last Whole Earth Catalog,* Jeanne Campbell described how, when she first arrived in California in 1972, with $120 to her name, she blew $50 of it on Gek's stamps.

The catalog went through a number of editions, and each reflected the surroundings it was created in or a personal event of significance. The April 1973 catalog bore earmarks of time spent with the land... with smatterings of old-fashioned landlore interspersed with the stamps.

Another catalog coincided with a birth in the family, and this, too, was part of the flow of the catalog. These early catalogs are treasured by those who have hung on to them.

The several hundred stamps and catalog now rest in the hands of Eileen Hitsky, a weaver, who continues onward with the fantastical contents, shown in the form of a giant newsprint broadside. "Step right up folks, get 'cha rubber stamp catalogue, volume 3, for you only 65¢."

Our suggestion would be to send for two copies of the catalog. The ordering procedure for this catalog is such that you clip out the image you want to buy and return it with the dough. If you get two, you can lacerate one for ordering purposes and maintain the other for the sheer pleasure of looking at it on your wall.

Stamp prices start at $3 for things like phrases that say *UNSAVORY* and *JIVE* or an image of a baseball catcher. For slightly more, you can end up with a cowgirl and a lasso or a joker perched on the moon with a pair of binoculars.

**ACE RUBBER STAMP & OFFICE SUPPLY CO.**
**135 The Arcade**
**Cleveland, Ohio 44114**

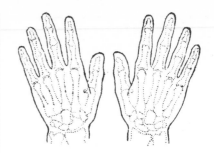

We've lumped the next four companies together due to the similarity of their special offerings. Each makes anatomical stamps, or, as United prefers to call them "Anatomical Diagram Plates" . . . an interesting euphemism for rubber stamps of left buccal mucosa, upper extremities, tops of heads, and side views of feet. Anatomical stamps are frequently used in teaching hospitals, X-ray departments, government institutions, and cancer centers. They represent a convenient way to illustrate body parts and relationships on medical records.

Anatomical stamps are nothing new. A news article in the *Stamp Trade News*, September 1922, reported that during World War I, stamp houses received an unprecedented amount of business as a result of the war effort, much of it in anatomical stamps. One house made up an order of ten thousand stamps showing seventeen different diagrams of the human anatomy. These stamps were sent to army recruiting stations where they were used on recruits' records. Thousands of the same stamps made their way to the battlefields of France where the wounded or diseased soldier had the source of his troubles rubber-stamped on his record card.

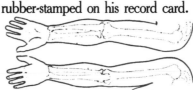

Although owner Don Lerner is new to the rubber-stamp business, his company has been around for a number of years. The dollar catalog of anatomical parts is one of his innovations. Over fifty stamps are shown; several of them are unusual. One is a male skeleton superimposed on top of a halftone body...all this on one stamp is simply amazing. Another shows four views of the human foot. You choose which foot. Prices for the stamps range from $0.90 to $1.20 per square inch with minimum charges for certain smaller ones. The manufacturing is top-quality and each is handle mounted.

Govin's brochure of anatomical stamps is free and shows over fifty stamps, each priced around $2.50. In the early days, the founding Govin, Armand, put signs on his 1928 Model A

**LEFT FOOT**

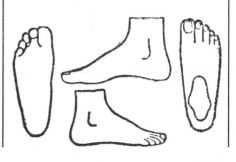

**RIGHT FOOT**

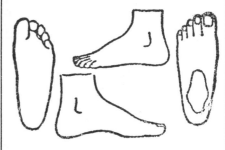

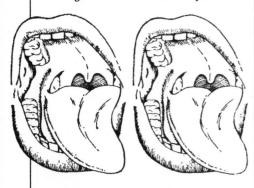

Coupe and drove around chasing business. His son, Ron, now heads the company and is also the current president of the Marking Device Association. The stamps are made of photopolymer, which lends itself very well to the fine details of anatomical drawings. Each is handsomely made

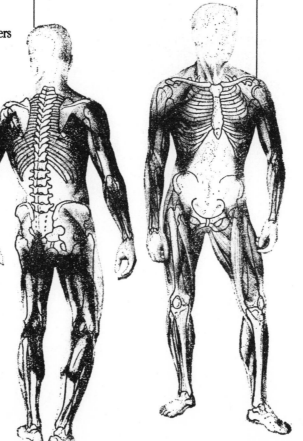

and comes with a varnished wood handle mount.

Sachs-Lawlor, "largest makers of marking products in the Rocky Mountain west," has been around since 1881. Drop them a postcard, and they'll shoot off their twenty-one-page anatomical rubber-stamp catalog free of charge. Watch for the prize finds —item S-118 is a craggy string of teeth (approx. $4.25), and the combination of items S-119 and S-120 (about $5 for the "set") will enable you to stamp wonderful two-inch-high ears on all manner of things that don't normally have them. The stamps are mounted on hardwood with a handle, and each has a "full-view celluloid covered label for easy identification." Average price is $3.50 per stamp.

United's "Anatomical Diagram Plates" are an off shoot of their regular business. The main thrust of the company is marketing medical products to hospitals and discharged patients who have undergone surgery. The designs come from surgeons, technicians, and cancer experts and each image was drawn by a qualified medical illustrator. Stamps are made to order with heavy clear plastic mounts and are considered a serious medical tool. Prices, around $16 per stamp, reflect their specialized nature. A professional-looking catalog of the plates is $1.50.

049

**BOOKMAN ENTERPRISE**
9476 North Street
La Rue, Ohio 43332

**DECOR-8-CRAFT PRODUCTS**
9635 Liberty School Road,
Route 5
Cambridge, Ohio 43725

**HOBBIES & THINGS**
30915 Lorain Road
North Olmsted, Ohio 44070

A handful of specialty rubber-stamp companies specialize in stamps designed for use in making note cards, stationery, and greeting cards. In general the designs are much less sophisticated then those from other kinds of stamp companies and lean heavily toward flowers, kittens, frogs, caricatures, and drawings of cute children in ruffled frocks. Don't let this stop you. There are some wonderful gems in these catalogs. Another plus is these companies sell most of their stamps both mounted and unmounted, which makes the prices very appealing.

Bookman Enterprise is the official name for this company but the catalog says "Betty's Brochure of Decorative Designs," a folksier name that more aptly reflects the type of designs. The selection in this $1 catalog is wide, over eight hundred, which means you have to look carefully for the prime choices, which include a merry-go-round, praying hands in a variety of sizes, some wonderful tree branches, and a very large, very Japanese-looking design of a cat's back. A portion of the catalog is labeled "Ruby's Rubber Stamp Collection" and it includes designs from the collection of Ruby Flynn, now deceased, who was one of the very first people to design and make rubber stamps specifically for decorating stationery and cards. The favorite here is a pair of coquettish-looking skeletons that are beyond

belief. Stamp prices average around $1.50 each.

If you have a passion for covered bridges, ask the Bookmans about their selection of over one hundred from Ruby Flynn's collection which are not shown in the catalog.

People have always liked to add decorations to their writing; if the decorated writing paper is made by hand, it is a craft," says Donald Allen. He and wife Mary offer a selection of over seven hundred designs in their catalog, which sells for $1. Prices range from $0.50 to $4 per stamp and you have a choice of ordering them mounted or unmounted. They have a wide selection of very sweet flower designs, several series meant to be used as teacher's grading stamps, and one big stamp of . . . The Last Supper.

The Allens are responsible for reviving an unusual method of using

*Letta Lettuce*

*Charlie Carrot*

*Cora Cabbage*

stamps for embossing. The process is a simple one: Make an impression with a rubber stamp using a special slow-drying ink, sprinkle embossing powder on the impression, blow off excess powder, and hold the paper up against a 100- or 150-watt light bulb. The same technique will work for embossing heavy cardboard or wood; the only difference is you bake the piece in the oven. The embossing powder comes in fourteen colors (including gold and silver). Both the vials of powder and a selection of

unusual stamp-pad ink colors (violet, brown, carnation pink) are listed in the catalog.

The Allens also offer a full line of special-order services and will make name-and-address stamps with designs from the catalog and convert any black-and-white design into a rubber stamp.

K aren Joseph got her start in the rubber-stamp business as a Decor-8-Craft stamp dealer and has since gone on to create her own $1 catalog of rubber stamps. The catalog includes a selection of Decor-8-Craft designs as well as many others. Unlike the Allens, who design their own stamps, Karen

relies on her customers to submit designs to be added to her line. If a design is accepted, she gives the artist a choice of a free stamp or its cash equivalent. Among the offerings are "Scripture Stamps" with quotes from the Bible, a very festive Christmas stocking, a baby grand piano, and an extensive variety of phrase stamps with little poems and ditties suitable for greeting cards, birth announcements, birthdays, anniversaries, etc.

Karen carries a complete line of embossing supplies as well as stamp pads in crazy colors like egg yellow, royal purple, and sky blue. She will also custom-make stamps.

One entire page of the catalog is devoted to blank stationery and cards including reasonably priced post-cards in nice colors (salmon, buff, etc.), blank business cards, and assortments of gift tags with strings.

Unmounted stamps start at $0.15, mounted ones $0.25, and you can request your stamps specially mounted on quarter-inch foam rubber for use on ceramics.

# RUBBER STAMP ABCEDARIAN

A stamp collection without at least one alphabet is like a bird without wings. "In the hands of an operator of reasonably good taste" (as one old stamp catalog puts it), alphabet stamps can be helpful in creating attention-getting envelopes, snappy-looking short-term signs, crystal-clear drawer labels, and peculiar name tags.

In their earliest incarnation, rubber-stamp alphabets were called sign markers and came neatly arranged in cardboard or leatherette boxes with tidy dividers to keep the letters from straying. Some were more lavishly ensconced in polished-wood carrying cases with small brass latches. The sets came with all the trimmings—ink pad, ink, ruler, and spacing guide.

Some of the first commercially-manufactured sign markers were produced by a fellow named Maxson who operated in both Chicago and New York just before 1890. Maxson neatly solved the problem of mounting italic alphabets by cutting the wooden molding on the diagonal, and these sets were very unusual looking.

Other early biggies in the sign-marker field were R.H. Smith Manufacturing Company, Springfield, Massachusetts ("Easy" and "Economy" sets); Superior Type Company, Chicago, Illinois; Hans Hellesoe, Chicago, Illinois ("Columbia"); Fulton Specialty Company, Elizabeth, New Jersey; Russel T. Hogg, Chicago, Illinois ("Aristocrate"); and W.T. Geisinger, Long Island City, New York, who sold sets under his own name to high-volume outlets like depart-

052

ment stores. Superior and Columbia sign markers are still manufactured today.

Traffic in sign markers accounted for a substantial portion of the early stamp business. There was hardly a shop owner who didn't use one daily "for making advertising signs that sell the goods." An early R.H. Smith Manufacturing Company catalog enumerates over fifty styles and sizes for use by dry-goods stores, school teachers, vegetable-stand owners, traveling salesmen, canvassers, and grocers.

Sunday-school charts and texts were often whipped up with sign markers. In the early 1930s, Louis Waynai of Los Angeles displayed his religious zeal and loving relationship to the Bible by spending two laborious years printing a monster-sized Bible with rubber stamps. It spread eight feet across, weighed 1,094 pounds, and contained 8,048 hand-stamped pages. No note is made of Waynai's mental health after completing this inspired project, but we have visions of him quietly sitting and babbling random biblical quotations.

There were specialty markers, too. Hebrew sign markers came into existence due to popular demand. When telegraphs and cables represented the fastest means of communication between two parties, R.H. Smith Manufacturing Company eased the lot of clerks by producing "Telegraph and Cable Code Sign Markers."

Many collectors' first interest in stamps was aroused by marker sets. Noted stamp personage and artist Ken Friedman gave credit to his grandfather Michael's set in his text prepared for the exhibition *Images From The Rubber Stamp Museum,* presented at La Mamelle in San Francisco in the fall of 1977. "My grandfather had a grocery store . . . over half a century ago. He used a set of old-fashioned marking stamps to prepare his signs and price labels. I was given that set of stamps in 1956, and from that time on have been interested in stamps." Friedman pointed out that the text in two well-known books, Baba Ram Dass's *Be Here Now* and Kaprow's *Assemblages, Environments and Happenings,* were both done with Superior's Universal Sign Marker set.

If the various rubber-stamp alphabets for sale don't do anything for you, consider having a distinctive alphabet of your choice custom made. Bear in mind that the cost is likely to be quite high, perhaps as much as three dollars per letter, so a sensible determination must be made about whether life can go on without an Algonquin Shaded or Morris Black alphabet. Dover Publications publishes some good books with ready-to-use black-and-white illustrations of a wide variety of alphabets. Merely pick an alphabet, clip the pages, and take them to a stamp company. The titles to look for are:

*French and Italian alphabets are mounted on wheel-like moldings. Two stamps equal a full alphabet.*

**053**

*Art Nouveau Display Alphabets: 100 Complete Fonts*, selected and arranged by Dan X. Solo, $3; *Victorian Display Alphabets: 100 Complete Fonts*, same author, $3; and *Historic Alphabets & Initials: Woodcut & Ornamental*, edited by Carol Belanger Grafton, $4.

Books like these will spare you the hassle W.H. Lohman of the Lohman Rubber Stamp Works in San Francisco endured to create his astonishing Chinese alphabet in the 1920s. Although he had studied Chinese for years, Lohman spent four years double-checking his information with local Chinese merchants before hand-engraving the wooden cuts used to create his Chinese alphabet of 214 roots of the written Chinese language. Such an endeavor qualifies more as a way of life than as a rubber-stamp alphabet.

To give the full scope of what is currently available for sale in the rubber-stamp alphabet ranks, we have pulled together a sampling of those currently being offered by various companies. Most are sold as sets, although some can be purchased a letter at a time. A few come boxed, some in cloth sacks. Many do not come with pads, inks, etc. Presumably you'll supply those yourself, unlike C.J. Fell's customer in Wilkesbarre, Pennsylvania, who complained of the abso-

## AaBbCcDdEeFf-67890
MARY ALICE SCENIC STAMPS™

## ABCDEF125
MARY ALICE SCENIC STAMPS™

## ABCDEFGHIJK123
MARY ALICE SCENIC STAMPS™

## ABC25
MARY ALICE SCENIC STAMPS™

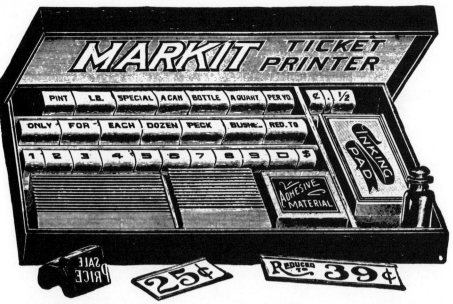

lute failure of his stamps to print. Mr. Fell "was most solicitous in discovering the source of trouble, which, in point of fact, did not take very long, since the purchaser first pressed the marker on his tongue for the wetting medium and then tried the stamp on paper." The customer was duly impressed when a stamp pad was used and the stamps miraculously worked.

AaBbCcDdEeFfGg 1234
MARY ALICE SCENIC STAMPS™

AaBbCcDd 25
MARY ALICE SCENIC STAMPS™

AaBbCcDd 25
MARY ALICE SCENIC STAMPS™

ABCD5
MARY ALICE SCENIC STAMPS™

HERO ARTS

GRAPHISTAMP™

MARY ALICE SCENIC STAMPS™

RUBBERSTAMPEDE

ABCDE

STAMP N'STITCH™

ALL NIGHT MEDIA

RUBBER STAMP CATALOGUE

A B C D E F G H I J K L

DECOR-8-CRAFT

RED RUBBER VALLEY

RUBBERSTAMPEDE

A B C D E F G H I J K L M N P

RED RUBBER VALLEY

ALL NIGHT MEDIA

057

# ERASERS THAT LEAVE A MARK

If you always thought erasers were only good for getting rid of mistakes, think again. Carved, they can be an interesting alternative to the standard rubber stamp.

Corita Kent, widely known for her unusual silk-screen serigraphs, taught students the finer points of eraser stamping in classes at Immaculate Heart College in Los Angeles, where she once headed the now-famous art department. Corita's stamp-carving days began in the early 1960s when one of her students brought in a complete alphabet to show her. Each letter had been carved on the eraser end of a pencil. As a feat of craftsmanship it has to rate right up there with engraving the heads of pins. Corita used her own eraser alphabets in three books—*Damn Everything but the Circus, To Believe in Man* and *To Believe in Things*—which are still available through Corita Prints, 5126 Vineland Avenue, North Hollywood, California 91601.

David Mekelburg, who has both studied and taught art at Immaculate Heart, is well known for his special calligraphy, drawings, and serigraphs. He is also an eraser-stamp expert. Ben Shahn said once "a stamp in the hand of an artist is calligraphy" and David adds, "especially when cut by the artist." On a later spread, we show David's instructions on how to carve images out of erasers, too. We thought his hand-stamped letter was so lovely and lucid that we would treat you to it in its entirety. The original is a two-page masterpiece each page a whopping 16½" x 22".

Most of the people we talked to use Eberhard-Faber Rubkleen Erasers, finding their texture particularly well-suited to carving, but other types of erasers will also work. Diane Merrill, a Mekelburg student, carved her first eraser in 1967 but didn't renew her acquaintance with eraser carving until she attended his design-calligraphy course taught in 1976. Her description of wielding an Exacto knife is endearing—"I am very comfortable with the knife, perhaps I am a frustrated surgeon or was one in a past life. I have never cut myself and like the feel of the tool and the meditative aspect of the cutting. When I am immersed in the process it is very soothing as the tip of the blade silently pulls through the smooth rubber."

Tools and materials for eraser stamps are very reasonable. An eraser runs about $0.75, an Exacto $1.25. You can even double up and carve a design on each side. Storage of the stamps is no problem

SISTER MARIE VINCENT BROTHERS

TEN YEARS AFTER I CARVED THIS ALPHABET IN CORITAS CLASS IT IS IN USE IN MY CLASSROOM AT ROSATI KAIN HIGH

SISTER MARIE VINCENT BROTHERS

ABCDEFGHIJKLM
NOPQRSTUVWX
YZabcdefghijklmn
opqrstuvwxyz

Riecken
9 Vincent St
Cambridge
Ma 02140

since erasers come in a few standard sizes and you don't have mountings to worry about. Susan Riecken keeps hers neatly stored in plastic ice-cube trays. This is especially handy for keeping alphabets in some semblance of order.

Artist Susan Riecken is a wizard with an eraser. Every speck of her annual publication, an engagement-calendar book of days, is stamped. For eight months of the year, Susan keeps a running record of things that strike her fancy or stir her imagination—bits of poetry, quotations from books she is reading, the fond memory of a convivial late-afternoon tea party. The more visual memories end up as designs carved out of Eberhard-Faber Rubkleen erasers. Exacto knives are her only tools. The resulting engagement calendar is breathtaking. Even the alphabets and numerals used are all carved erasers. The text is stamped out with them before being reproduced by a mechanical offset-printing process. The real kicker is that each of the twenty-six or so illustrations is actually *hand* stamped, not printed, on the pages. With helpers pulling pages as she goes, Susan positions each eraser on a specially inked pad and then stamps away. Some of the impressions are made with as many as four colors and the effects range from a simple, jolly pair of red mittens to an iris of misted delicacy in shadings of blue, purple, and green. Each is a miniature work of art. The inks are painted in strips on uninked foam pads to match up with various portions of each design.

The calendar has some nice, useful touches—an inscription page, a paper pocket at the back for storing bits of paper you don't want to lose track of, and a bibliography with commentary on the quotations. The calendar sells out earlier each year. The first one in 1972 was a limited twenty-five-copy edition, the 1978 one a three thousand-copy edition. The best way to make sure you get one is to put yourself on Susan's mailing list by sending a stamped, self-addressed envelope. Each September she advises those on the list about details of the new calendar. The cost is modest, around $7 per calendar.

Susan also accepts commissions and has designed everything from violin recital programs to wedding and birth announcements with her eraser stamps. Hand-made notecards are also available in a variety of stamped designs. Our favorites—a chubby teapot with a heart and a heart-in-hand. Each package contains ten notecards and envelopes for about $4.

JUNE – JULY

25 SUNDAY

26 MONDAY

27 TUESDAY

28 WEDNESDAY

29 THURSDAY

30 FRIDAY

1 SATURDAY

The whole afternoon in my memory is hung with swags of strawberries.

Katherine Mansfield

# Dear Joni,

I AM SORRY THAT THIS IS SO LATE BUT THERE HAS NOT BEEN ENOUGH TIME TO WRITE *or stamp* ANYTHING FOR YOU.

I CARVE MY OWN RUBBER STAMP ALPHABETS FROM ERASERS. IT IS A SUPERB WAY TO STUDY AND TEACH LETTERING. HERE ARE JUST A FEW SAMPLE STYLES:

ABCabcde
**ABCDE**
abcdefgh
**ABCD**
**ABCDE**
**ABCDEF**
**ABCD**
**ABCDE**

I USE RUBKLEEN GREEN ERASERS AND NUMBER ELEVEN EXACTO KNIVES. I USED TO DRAW THE LETTERS ON THE ERASERS BUT NOW I SIMPLY PHOTOCOPY ALPHABETS FROM TYPE BOOKS. IF YOU USE A WET-PROCESS COPYING MACHINE THE LETTERS WILL TRANSFER VERY NICELY TO THE ERASERS WITH A LITTLE RUBBING. USE A SCISSORS, HANDLE AND HOLD THE TRANSFER SHEET FIRMLY IN PLACE AND BE SURE TO GET ALL OF THE LETTER IMAGE TRANSFERRED TO THE ERASER. CAREFUL WORK IS ESSENTIAL IF YOU WANT SHARP LETTER STAMPS.[1]

1. MOST OF THE MACHINES IN STORES AND MARKETS ARE THE RIGHT KIND.

USE THE TIP OF THE BLADE TO MAKE SHARP CUTS ABOUT ONE SIXTEENTH OF AN INCH DEEP. CUT STRAIGHT DOWN - NOT AT AN ANGLE - OR THE EDGES OF THE LETTERS WILL NOT PRINT CLEARLY. VERY GENTLY PEEL AWAY THE RUBBER INSIDE AND AROUND THE LETTER SHAPES. THE LAST STEP IS TO TRIM THE ERASER TO THE SHAPE AND SIZE OF THE LETTER SO THAT YOU CAN SEE WHAT YOU ARE DOING WHEN STAMPING AND SPACING YOUR WORDS.

I AM A CALLIGRAPHER AND TYPOGRAPHER BUT I HAVE DESIGNED QUITE A FEW GREETING CARDS, BOOK COVERS AND PAGES WITH MY RUBBER STAMPS. THEY CREATE A UNIQUE TEXTURE GIVING A SPECIAL FEEL TO THE MESSAGE OR STATEMENT. SOME PRINTED EXAMPLES ARE ENCLOSED.

# Good luck with the book.

David Mekelburg

DAVID MEKELBURG

THIS IS WHAT YAHWEH ASKS OF YOU: TO ACT JUSTLY TO LOVE TENDERLY AND TO WALK HUMBLY WITH YOUR GOD

MICHEA 6:8

SISTER MARY GEROLD MOBLEY

carve five
this week
corita said
and i had to
choose one
with curves

SISTER MARIE VINCENT BROTHERS

# CORITA'S RULES & HINTS
## for students and teachers

**ONE** FIND A PLACE YOU TRUST AND THEN TRY TRUSTING IT FOR A WHILE

**TWO** GENERAL DUTIES OF A STUDENT—PULL EVERYTHING OUT OF YOUR TEACHER, PULL EVERYTHING OUT OF YOUR FELLOW STUDENTS

**THREE** GENERAL DUTIES OF A TEACHER—PULL EVERYTHING OUT OF YOUR STUDENTS

**FOUR** CONSIDER EVERYTHING AN EXPERIMENT

**FIVE** be self disciplined THIS MEANS FINDING SOMEONE WISE OR SMART AND CHOOSING TO FOLLOW THEM. TO BE DISCIPLINED IS TO FOLLOW IN A GOOD WAY TO BE SELF DISCIPLINED IS TO FOLLOW IN A BETTER WAY

**SIX** NOTHING IS A MISTAKE. THERE'S NO WIN AND NO FAIL. THERE'S ONLY MAKE

**SEVEN** THE ONLY RULE IS WORK. IF YOU WORK IT WILL LEAD TO SOMETHING. IT'S THE PEOPLE WHO DO ALL OF THE WORK ALL THE TIME WHO EVENTUALLY CATCH ON TO THINGS

**EIGHT** DON'T TRY TO CREATE AND ANALYSE AT THE SAME TIME. THEY'RE DIFFERENT PROCESSES

**NINE** BE HAPPY WHENEVER YOU CAN MANAGE IT. ENJOY YOURSELF. IT'S LIGHTER THAN YOU THINK

**TEN** "WE'RE BREAKING ALL OF THE RULES. EVEN OUR OWN RULES AND HOW DO WE DO THAT? BY LEAVING PLENTY OF ROOM FOR X QUANTITIES" JOHN CAGE

## HELPFUL HINTS
ALWAYS BE AROUND. COME OR GO TO EVERYTHING. ALWAYS GO TO CLASSES. READ ANYTHING YOU CAN GET YOUR HANDS ON. LOOK AT MOVIES CAREFULLY OFTEN. SAVE EVERYTHING. IT MIGHT COME IN HANDY LATER

*Corita's "Rules and Hints" were thought up on a California field trip with Immaculate Heart students in 1967. An eleventh rule - "Every once in a while throw out all the rules and make new ones - or learn how to do it without rules" -was added later.*

# MAKE A GOOD IMPRESSION

Early stamp pads were awful . . . the inks used were terrifically smelly. The pads themselves were made of gelatin which degenerated into a gooey mess during hot weather. They drew insects like bees to honey.

Stamp-pad pioneer B.G. Volger was a buffalo-robe salesman when he chanced to encounter, on a train, in 1880 a fellow named Baumgarten whose sideline was making stamp pads. Baumgarten poured gelatin into tin boxes, impregnated the gelatin with dyestuff, and covered it with fabric. Resourceful Baumgarten is said to have checked out of hotels taking sheets from the bed with him which he thriftily tore into strips and used as pad coverings. In 1884 Volger entered the business, creating his Excelsior Stamp Pad (two felts and a blotter on a wooden base covered with nainsook). His pads were typically vile smelling, but in 1908, after five years of experimenting, he perfected a formula for quick-drying, nonsmear ink and eliminated the awful odor so characteristic of early pads.

Two others were in the vanguard of stamp-pad manufacturing. In 1881, R.A. Stewart purchased the patent for gelatin self-inking pads and was the first to make them commercially available. His wife laboriously manufactured the pads in her kitchen. Alonzo Woodruff, cousin of James Orton Woodruff (probable inventor of the rubber stamp), started the Superb Stamp Pad Company in 1891 and devoted years to perfecting a variety of well-known stamp pads.

Here is a rundown on the basic types of stamp pads available today:

CARTER'S ® MICROPORE ® STAMP PADS: We recommend this unique pad above all others for extremely high-quality, fine impressions. The pad itself is rather odd looking—the result of a patented formula which is carefully guarded. Carter's describes the pad as consisting of "millions of microscopic ink beads blended in a porous plastic that gives a continuous fountain of ink." Micropores ® can't be re-inked, and the colors lack intensity, so you do make a trade-off to achieve the superior impressions they make. They come in two sizes (small for around $2, large for about $2.75) and in five colors—black, blue, red, green, and purple. Carter's ® considers them a "commercial" product as opposed to one manufactured for everyday use by ordinary people, so their availability is often scarce. Look for them in office-supply stores and very large, completely-stocked stationery stores. If that fails, you can order them through the mail from Bizzaro Rubber Stamp Catalog in Providence, Rhode Island.

A word of caution—Carter's ® also makes felt and foam stamp pads with practically identical packaging. Many stores will unwittingly give you those instead of a Mic-

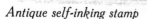

*Antique self-inking stamp*

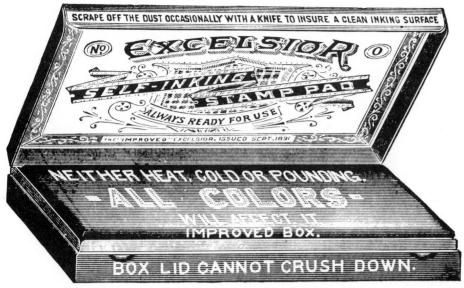

ropore ® when you ask, so always double-check to make sure you got what you asked for.

FELT STAMP PADS: These are the most common pads made, and they can be found absolutely everywhere—dime-stores, stationery stores, corner variety stores, commercial rubber-stamp companies, and sometimes even in drugstores. They consist of a thick felt base covered with fabric, come in four sizes (costing between $1.35 and $4.75) and five colors—black, blue, red, green, and purple. They are sturdy, last a long time, and can be re-inked with any ink labeled "rubber stamp-pad ink." Everybody and his dog makes this type of pad, and, with the exception of the Stafford brand pads, we haven't been able to discern any real difference between one brand and another. Stafford pads make extremely good impressions, and the colors have unusual intensity.

Two companies listed in the catalog section (Decor-8-Craft and Hobbies and Things) offer felt pads in a wide variety of unusual colors.

Felt pads are also available uninked for use with specialty inks such as indelible ink. It's always handy to have several of these in reserve for those times in the middle of the night when you are moved to start stamping your sheets or decorating your socks.

FOAM STAMP PADS: Just as common as felt pads, these are made of foam rubber and come in the same standard sizes and colors that felt pads do. Once again there's no discernible difference among the various brands. They cost slightly less than felt pads and can be found in the same places. We are not big fans of foam pads. It is often difficult to get an even distribution of ink on the stamp's surface with foam. They do, however, work well for inking stamps carved from erasers which need to sink into a stamp-pad surface for an even distribution of ink. Re-ink them with "rubber stamp-pad ink." They are available uninked and do work well in tandem with meat-marking (edible) inks.

WOOD STAMP PADS: These are really strange. Our friend Martin Brophy, who runs Fulton Specialty in Elizabeth, New Jersey, swears they are the perfect stamp pad. At least two companies make them—Fulton and Phillips Process Company, Rochester, New York —each claiming that a special process used in their manufacture makes them unique.

Phillips Process Company describes theirs as "a block of specially processed wood with the grain exposed." After special chemical treatment, the grain of the wood acts as a series of reservoirs holding a large amount of ink. Due to capillary attraction these reservoirs feed just the right amount of ink to the surface. These wood pads come inked in black, red, blue, purple, green, or brown. The ink dries instantly, leaving a waterproof impression. Phillips' George Richards says you can put a piece of paper into water on the bottom of a pan, ink your stamp on one of their wood pads, quickly lower the stamp through the water, and make a perfect impression on the paper at the bottom. Try it, it's kind of fun.

This type of pad must be re-inked with special inks; each pad costs around $2, and they are harder to find than other pads. Some

**0 6 8**

commercial stamp companies stock them or you can order the Phillips Process ones direct from them (address listed further on).

Another type of wood pad is available uninked (usually not specially treated) and is made from balsa wood. It can be used with edible or opaque inks.

## GENERAL INK INFORMATION

Specialty inks make it possible to use stamps on practically any surface . . . leather, cloth, plastic, food, skin, glass, porcelain, wood, waxed paper, chinaware, cellophane, metal, etc.

Ink manufacturers try to make their lines unique, often tailoring them for use with only their type of pad or special cleaning concoction. This makes it difficult to provide very specific advice on inks. Mainly we'd like to make you aware of the potential of inks by highlighting the basic types. Help in making the final choice, and specific instructions, should come from the companies themselves.

Two friendly, reliable ink manufacturers to contact are Phillips Process Company, Inc., 192 Mill Street, Rochester, New York 14614 (phone: 716-232-1825) and S.H. Quint Sons Company, Inc., 27 Letitia Street, Philadelphia, Pennsylvania 19106 (phone: 215-925-4044). The bulk of their business is done with commercial companies but they are very helpful to individuals. Phillips will send a multipage descriptive listing of inks if you send them a stamped, self-addressed envelope. If you already have a project in mind, include the details with your request—color ink you want, color and kind of material you wish to mark (a sample is helpful but not essential). Quint doesn't have a brochure but will respond to specific inquiries. Don Shaw of Quint says his job is "like being a doctor" only he is called a "marking specialist."

All commercial stamp companies stock at least some specialty inks or can order them, but you won't find them especially keen to spend a lot of time giving detailed advice and help.

## BASIC SPECIALTY INKS

FINGERPRINT: Comes in black, is especially fast drying, and washes off easily. Unlikely you'll have much use for this except as a party gag. Use with a special wooden pad covered with treated silk, or an uninked felt pad.

INDELIBLE: Also called "laundry" ink. Comes in black and is commonly available in

THE HANDY DATER

dime-stores, stationery stores, and commercial rubber stamp companies. Used mainly by hospitals and the military for laundry markings, it is excellent for stamping on fabrics, especially cotton and linen. Use with an uninked felt pad. Lovely effects can be achieved by coloring in stamped impressions on fabric with colored Magic Markers (the ones intended for permanent use on fabrics).

INVISIBLE: Use brand-new rubber stamps that have never been used with any other ink. Stamping will be invisible until object (or portion of the anatomy) is exposed to a blacklight. Use with uninked felt pad.

OPAQUE: This is a tricky one to work with. It is thick (more like paint than ink) and often appears "cakey" when dry. Opaque ink doesn't work well on fine detail stamps as it tends to clog fine lines quickly. Definitely ask for advice before using this type of ink. Comes in a wide variety of colors (everything you can imagine including silver and gold) and in special formulas to mark on metal, plastic, mylar, polyethlene, glass, ceramics, and even resin-coated photographic paper.

Some brands should be used with uninked wooden pads; others work best with special opaque pads which are sold in pairs. Each pad is a felt block, mounted on wood, with a fabric covering. Stroke the ink onto one half and then rub the two pads face to face for even ink distribution. When storing the pads, put them face to face, held together with a rubber band, to avoid drying and caking of the ink.

Always use this ink in a well-ventilated work space—it has a very powerful smell.

Some opaque inks are designed for use on waxed paper and cellophane. Cellophane gift wrap would be quite spiffy wrapped around gifts of potted plants or homemade food.

Make sure your stamps are squeaky clean; otherwise the impressions made will be muddy looking.

MEAT BRANDING: Also called "edible" ink. It's a one hundred percent edible, water soluble, nontoxic vegetable dye manufactured to meet government standards. Can safely be used on skin and food. Most common color is purple, but it's also made in green, black, and red.

Commercial rubber-stamp companies usually have only purple in stock but can order the other colors. Bizzaro Rubber Stamp Catalog in Providence, Rhode Island, sells it through their catalog. Use with an uninked foam or felt pad.

PARACHUTE: Designed specifically for use by the government for parachute marking, it works best on nylon and will withstand normal washings. Not for use on anything that will be dry-cleaned. Has a strong, distinctive odor and takes a long time to dry. Colors include black, white, blue, yellow, green, and red. Use with an uninked wood or felt pad.

Choice of paper (and quality of the resulting impressions) depends on the quality of the stamp itself and the type of ink or pad used. Generally, the smoother the paper, the better the impression. Moisture and humidity tend to make even the best paper soggy, and images will be fuzzy.

We've used some mildly fancy jargon here which might come in handy when communicating with the person in the art supply store.

Plate (hot-pressed) finish Bristol Board in any weight is good and chrome-coated paper is excellent.

Acetate works well if the ink is allowed to dry overnight. Stamp the shiny side—never use the frosted one.

Vellum-quality tracing paper is extremely smooth and takes good impressions but less expensive tracing papers are likely to take fuzzy impressions.

Bond paper is the most common, readily-available paper, and it'll take a nice, clear impression. Ledger bond is even smoother, with a hard finish, and takes very good impressions.

Newsprint tends to be rough so images will have fuzzy edges.

Regular tissue paper (the slick side) takes good impressions, and shiny surfaced shelf paper works splendidly.

Whatever you do, don't use erasable typing paper—the impressions will bleed into obscurity in only a few days.

Regardless of the type of paper you choose, you'll get a better impression if you slip a magazine under it to provide a cushioned surface. It's also helpful to use moderate pressure when inking a stamp. If you grind or thump the stamp on a pad you won't get an even distribution of ink on the stamp surface.

You can make an image look like it's in motion by dragging a stamp across paper without lifting up . . . or you can drag it in an arc for even more unusual results.

To make a partial impression of a stamp, mask an area of the paper you plan to stamp with a second sheet of paper. Stamp away. The resulting impression will appear part on the mask, part on the paper you wanted to stamp. Voila! There's the body with no head!!

Experiment . . . choosing the best combination of paper and ink depends on your stamps. What works with one stamp, may not work with another. Get to know your stamps and their idiosyncrasies.

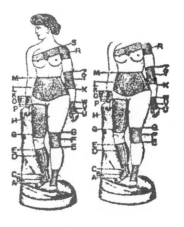

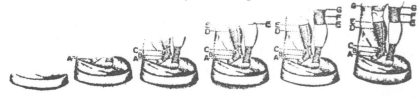

# STAMP HYGIENE

Somewhere between furiously cleaning a stamp each time it is used and never giving a thought to its condition, lies a happy medium of hygiene that is worth paying attention to if you want your stamps to last as long as you do.

One thing is a must. Always keep a blank piece of paper handy and drag the stamp across the paper immediately after use to quickly remove leftover ink. This makes serious cleaning later less of a hassle. Some regime of whole-hog cleaning is desirable because when ink is allowed to build up on stamps over a long period of time, it will eventually result in fuzzy, fading impressions.

Dirty stamps make switching stamp-pad colors a hazardous proposition. This is critical when using Carter's™ Micropore™ pads since they easily retain whatever previous color ink was on your stamp. It is very disappointing to go for a good, clear, fertile green on a tree and end up with some awful, murky in-between color. If you intend to use your stamps with opaque inks and pads, a perfectly clean stamp-surface is a must.

The following methods will all work, some more thoroughly than others.

Always clean stamps over a sink or a protected work surface so there is no chance the cleaning mess can stain counters or whatever.

Never attempt to clean stamps with any solvent that contains oil. Oil is the kiss of death to rubber.

TOOTHBRUSH METHOD: After each use, wipe excess ink off with a cloth and gently scrub surface of the rubber with an old, dry toothbrush. Or dip your aged toothbrush in a gentle mixture of lukewarm water and mild soap (Ivory Liquid is ideal) and lightly scrub the rubber. Do not put the entire stamp under a faucet or dunk the whole stamp directly into water. This will affect the wooden molding and may loosen the glue used to adhere the rubber to it. The only exception to this is "Clearstamps,™" which will remain unharmed when cleaned under running water.

In our opinion, the toothbrush method is the only totally safe way to clean stamps made of photo-polymer.

COMMERCIAL CLEANERS: There are a number of commercial stamp cleaners available through rubber-stamp companies and stationery and office-supply stores. Lee Products' A to Z™ Stamp Cleaner or Phillips' Merritone® solvent are good ones to try. Our luck with commercial cleaners has been mixed. They *do* clean thoroughly but can dissolve the glue holding the rubber to the molding. Use them with care. Cost is generally around $2 per bottle.

*Do not use commercial cleaners on photo-polymer stamps.* The solvents they contain may damage the stamps.

PLAIN OLD DENATURED ALCOHOL: This is what most

commercial stamp makers recommended when we asked them. It is inexpensive and readily available at hardware stores. Dampen a soft rag with denatured alcohol and rub or pat the rubber surface.

ORDINARY NAIL POLISH REMOVER: Jackie Leventhal of Hero Arts thought this method up. It works extremely well and is singularly unmessy. Dip a soft rag or a paper towel in nail polish remover and rub gently over rubber surface. The stamp will be clean in seconds.

*Leavenworth Jackson cleaning her stamps.*

# LIVING WITH YOUR STAMPS

The question of how to house your stamps when they're not in use can be a thorny one. There is no totally perfect method of storage that will comfortably accommodate all styles of stamp moldings at one time in one place. It is likely you'll opt for a combination of storage methods.

Leonore Fleischer, stamp collector extraordinaire, keeps her collection of over three thousand under wraps in plastic shoe boxes. These boxes cost between $0.75 and $1.25 at most variety, hardware, and dime stores. She marks each box with a general label—cartoon characters, birds, erotica, etc. Cartoonist Art Spiegelman, who also favors plastic boxes, makes impressions of the stamps on a file card and puts the card in the end of each box so he can tell what is what inside.

Plastic or metal fishing-tackle boxes will sometimes work, but be careful when choosing one since the little compartments are often too small for anything but the tiniest stamps.

Mail-art personage Ed Plunkett puts a hole in the top of the molding or handle of his stamps, puts a screw-eye in, and hangs them on cup hooks screwed into the underside of bookshelves. Stamps stored this way look cozy and are very handy to just reach up and pluck down. The idea of a screw-eye protruding out of the top of your stamp may hinder your stamping technique, however.

Commercial stamp companies generally carry or can order three basic types of storage units.

A revolving rack is the most common. It's designed to hold handle-mounted stamps and doesn't work well for molding ones. Capacity ranges from six to forty stamps.

For storing molding stamps, try a table-top rack with adjustable partitions.

*Pictured opposite is Gene Borckardt with his display of stamps at the original Flim-Flam Shop.*

Strip racks and single clips are cheap and effective if you have the wall space for them and aren't disturbed by holes in your walls. They fit on walls, the sides of tables, even inside desk drawers.

Of course, all these gimmicks cost money and you may want to buy more stamps instead.

Depending on how finicky you feel, you can really throw your stamps into practically anything—baskets, tea cannisters, wooden fruit crates, old tins, the lids of cardboard boxes, egg cartons, and so on.

# STAMP IT!

**S**tamps can make practically anything zanier, eye-catching and more distinctive.

This chapter is meant to give you a sampling of the multitude of things that can be attacked by your stamp collection.

So grab your stamps and go to it. . .

Stamping lunch bags is a splendid emotional outlet which allows you to inflict your mood with clarity on someone else's day. This can also be achieved in sneakier ways, such as stamping veiled threats on hardboiled eggs . . . or amorous miscellany on certain fruits. Children will feel extra special (grown-ups, too) if their lunch proclaims HAPPY BIRTHDAY.

Bet it never occurred to you that anything you stamp out on paper you can stamp out on a puzzle. Ah, yes, puzzles. A great way to confound acquaintances, they are especially valued when received by a bored convalescent going stir-crazy in a sickbed. You'll need stamps, of course, and some blank puzzles.

Drop a postcard to Lillian Vernon,™ 510 South Fulton Avenue, Mt. Vernon, New York 10550, and ask for the latest free catalog. Mixed in with a lot of other stuff, you'll find a listing for "intriguing jigsaw letters." For a pittance (around $3 per set) you can order either of two varieties—letter-sized squares or heart-shaped puzzles. They are made of blank white cardboard, come six to a set, and an envelope is included for each puzzle. All you have to do is stamp your message, break the puzzle apart, stuff it in the envelope, and speed it off to the lucky party. The more detailed and involved the stamping, the more nerve-wracking and suspenseful it will be for the poor soul trying to put the thing back together. Reconstructing the heart puzzle can be a particularly trying experience.

The puzzles would make crazy favors for a kid's birthday extravaganza, or really insane party invitations.

Early Valentines were handmade, and that still is the nicest way to show you care. Way back when, if you couldn't think of quite the right thing to say on your cards, you could turn for help to something called a "Valentine Writer," which was a booklet of verses especially designed to aid the inarticulate and lovelorn. A workable idea now for those times when flowery little nothings just don't leap to mind. Case the local card shop for ideas, rush back, and duplicate them with stamps. Even better yet, cadge ideas from antique postcards. Resurrecting the ideas is child's play with rubber stamps.

Around the turn of the century, "installment cards" were frequently sent to children—a series of postcards, one each day, over a period of

three or four days. Each card bore a portion of the total design or message and, when the final card arrived, the whole idea emerged.

Postcards were first introduced in the mid-1800s as a means of simplifying correspondence. Today they remain an artful way to appear thoughtful while writing as little as possible. Postcards sent out on a regular basis are the best defense for avoiding uncomfortable confrontations about how lousy you are about keeping in touch. They are also a convenient way to celebrate Leap Year, commemorate personal feats of daring, or honor the Great Pumpkin. The need for words is scant since you can leave the more substantive stuff to your stamps. Harass someone you're fond of by sending a postcard a day for months on end. There is endless potential for all kinds of foolish gestures in the postcard area.

Bizzaro makes a 🎀POST CARD🎀 stamp that makes transforming any sturdy piece of paper into a postcard a cinch. Decor-8-Craft also make a couple. If you plan to make postcards totally from scratch, keep in mind United States Postal requirements: minimum size is 3"x4¼", maximum is 4¼"x6". They plain won't accept anything smaller, and if you go over the maximum size, the post office will accept the card but require you use first-class postage.

Rubber-stamp alphabet sets can be an endless source of joy, inspiration, and functional fun. You'll find yourself stamping out dozens of nonessential signs for the sheer amusement of doing so. Hassled parents may find that communication with untidy children becomes more masterful and immediate when the child is confronted with a large, imposing-looking stamped sign. Deny rights, warn people off, or invite them in with stamped signs. Temporary signs can be done up handsomely on any kind of paper or poster board. If something more permanent is desired, stamp a board and varnish it after the stamping has had plenty of time to dry.

Sometimes labeling everything in sight can be a very comforting project. Right up there on a par with buying something you can't afford or pigging-out on a favorite food. Use images if you're feeling obscure, or come right out and call a box of household junk A BOX OF HOUSEHOLD JUNK.

When stamping on those shiny, adhesive-backed blank labels that are available all over the landscape, just make sure to allow plenty of time for the ink to dry. Overnight is best.

Defacing public monuments—in a nice way, of course—can be as easy as putting your stamps in your pocket. There is no point in leaving home without at least one or two whose sole purpose is to save you the trouble of drawing a moustache or a pair of lips.

If sexist signs and advertisements have you gritting your teeth, wage war with a THIS DEFILES WOMEN stamp!

Of course, your technique in these situations must be subtle. There is simply no point in stalking up to a sign on a bus or train and letting loose in front of thirty other passengers who may turn you in. The technique of cupping a stamp in the palm of the hand and sidling over to your target is a relatively simple one that can be refined with a little practice.

With stamps in your clutches, the need to clutter up closets with oddball assortments of special-occasion wrapping papers vanishes. One never has a suitable paper at the time it's needed anyway. Think back on the number of times you have blushingly wrapped a Father's Day gift in baby-shower paper or given a Christmas present that said "Happy Birthday." Smooth-surfaced shelf paper, Japanese rice paper, and brown kraft paper are

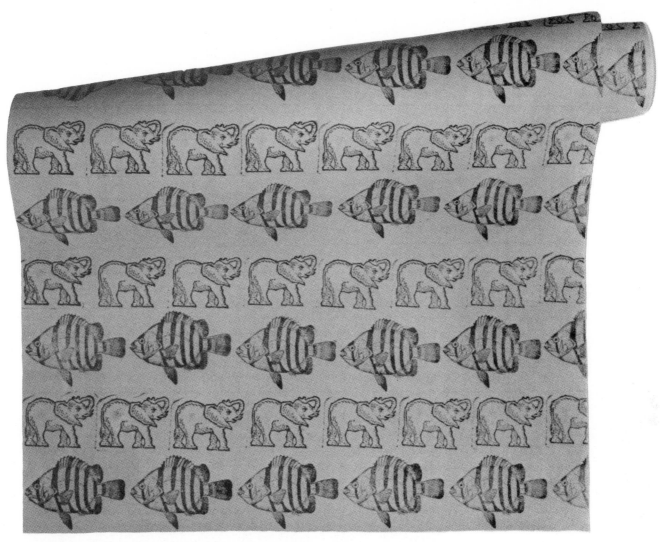

all suitable, and tissue paper is fantastic to stamp on.

Store-bought gift wrap never comes with enough gift cards. It's like getting eight hotdogs and only having six buns. Rubber stamps insure this can never happen again. The same stamp that made the paper, makes the card, too.

Try stamping out some flash cards if you are struggling through the rigors of learning a new language. You'll automatically absorb knowledge by having spent the time making them. Foreign-language teachers are always cheerily suggesting you tack the words for common objects on the objects themselves, as a way to gain constant exposure to vocabulary while wandering through your abode.

Communications arriving in envelopes that have been decorated in some substantial way with rubber stamps command instant attention and invariably arouse curiosity. The plain, bare-faced white envelope is the curse of the universe. A word of experienced caution about one thing—be careful about using rubber stamps of pointing hands on envelopes. The post office may confuse your stamp with theirs and zip it right back to you.

The arrival of the daily mail can be a bland event involving nothing more than the receipt of a few paltry bills and a packet of miscellaneous coupons for plastic billfolds and off-brand pantyhose, or it can be a diverting visual event. Just because most envelopes and stationery are born plain is no reason they should remain so. One owes it to friends and lovers to interject a note of gaiety and spunk into personal correspondence. John Morley once observed letters were "the most delightful waste of time," so any time spent giving them oomph is certainly worthwhile.

If the last letter you can remember writing was when you were eight and at camp, and it was executed under the eagle eye of an adolescent counselor, you'll find yourself quickly transformed into an inspired, if not positively lyrical, correspondent with stamps. It's cheap, too. Why bother to buy stationery when several swift whacks with a rubber stamp result in unique, personalized paper? You get what you want instantly. When was the last time you went into a store and bought stationery with a band of chickens or a pot roast or a peapod or an enormous cricket?

A packet of home-stamped stationery makes a good gift, especially if you are self-sacrificing enough to include the stamps used to make it as part of the gift. On pages that follow are some samples that should stir you to great heights. And here is the famous (??) GET A FINGER IN THIS PIE, designed by Lowry Thompson, which was sent to hundreds of unsuspecting stamp nuts during the course of compiling this book.

# GET A FINGER IN THIS

Hardened bill collectors, rich uncles, restive loan sharks, frantic creditors, and fretful dentists will find your late payments downright winsome when they arrive cunningly stamped.

If you failed to receive a single requested item from last year's Christmas list, you should reconsider the way you expressed your greed. Was the list a tacky one on hand-scrawled bits of scrap paper? Not a very effective way to ask for a sugar daddy, a little hideaway in the South of France, or even a modestly priced subscription to *Time* magazine!

Such situations call for forceful language and powerful graphics. Unless you wish to be surprised with three cheese assortments from

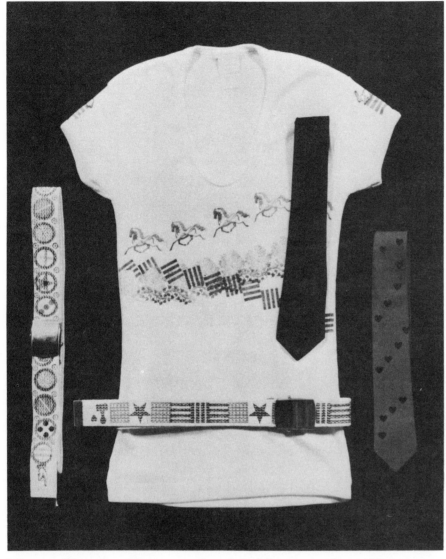

*Decorated clothing designed by Joanne Hoffman.*

Harry & David, a lifetime supply of dark-brown socks or fifteen rose-bud-shaped guest soaps, it pays to be firm, highly specific . . . and *graphic.*

It's a sad (but true) fact that most people find it hard, if not downright impossible, to get themselves in gear to send a simple thank-you note.

This can be the result of outright sloth, or it can be due to a certain reluctance to commit to writing how much you loved those plastic, fruit-shaped refrigerator magnets or the handknit socks with six toes.

Aha. The dilemma is solved in a flash with a rubber stamp alphabet and a single stamp from Patrick & Co. in San Francisco. THE ULTIMATE MAKE-IT-IN-FIVE-MINUTES-AND-BE -A-HERO THANK-YOU LETTER was invented by Joni Miller, who actually has plastic, fruit-shaped magnets on her you-know-what and likes them.

# DEAR JURIS,

THANKS THANKS THANKS THANKS THANKS THANKS THANKS THANKS

BABY

BEV TONDREAU

JONI K. MILLER

082

083

YOU ARE HERE

stationery·cards·bookmarks...

MOLLY'S
PLACE

MAY NOTHING
EVER COME
BETWEEN US
TO CUT OUR
FRIENDSHIP

# AT LAST

**Business Reply Mail**

No postage necessary if mailed in the United States

Postage will be paid by:

**State National**
BANK OF CONNECTICUT
P. O. Box 1049
Bridgeport, Conn. 06601

STATE EDUCATION DEPARTMENT

# CHICKEN SCRATCH

the rubber stan
joni mille
318 south av
new canaan, ct.

Come on over
and set awhile

TINA DAVIS

*Tina Davis' inexpensive solution to a builder's stationery was to design a stamp logo to be used on graph paper. Also shown, her own  valentine.*

wrapping paper ...

CHEAP
GIFT

CHEAP
GIFT

CHEAP
GIFT

CHEAP
GIFT

LOWRY THOMPSON

PLEASE...
slam door when
running
away from
home !!!

signs ...

sssshhhh!
baby sleeps

A  WITHOUT

A IS LIKE

A WITHOUT

A

MENS ROOM

LOWRY THOMPSON

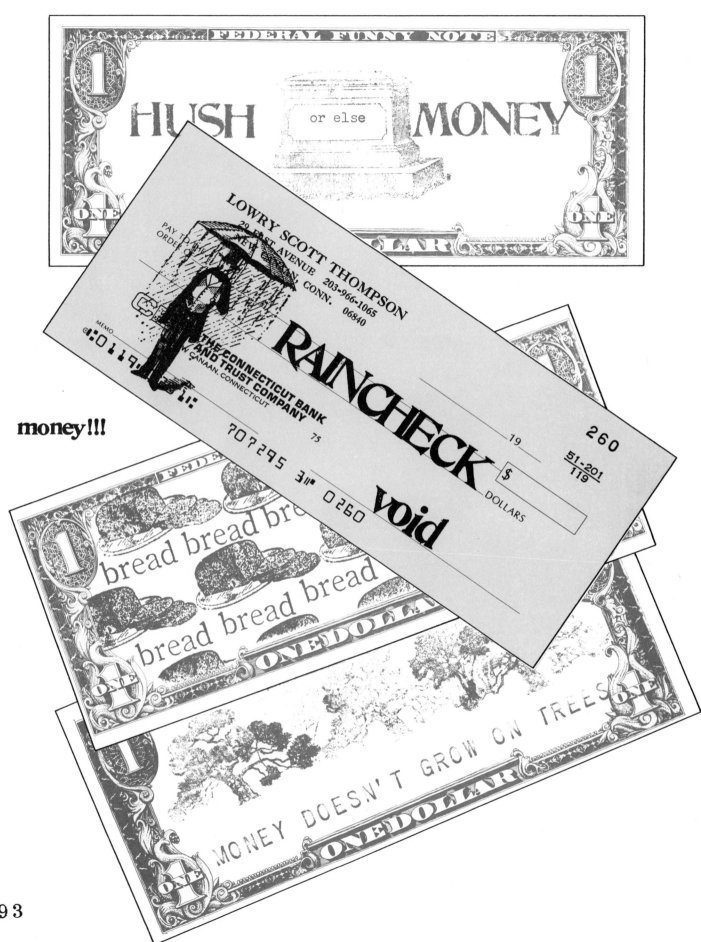

money!!!

# Courant

## !!! DANGER !!!

**By Annalise Masten**

The alcohol seminars this year were presented in part by someone new. Lou Berizzi is the new person. He's from the National Council on Alcoholism which has several locations in the area.

The N.C.A. is not the same as Alcoholics Anonymous. A.A. is a group of alcoholics who have agreed they have a problem with alcohol, and are trying to do something about it. The N.C.A. is a referral service. If you have any problem dealing with alcohol, whether it's that your parent drinks too much or that you suspect that a close friend is an alcoholic, you can call the N.C.A. and they will tell you where to go to get help.

Another group mentioned was Alateen. John Neikerk spoke about Alateen, which is a group situation like A.A. whose purpose is to make it easier for other people in a family to live with their alcoholic parent. Living with an alcoholic can be one of the toughest experiences anyone can face, and Alateen trys to make it a little easier by telling you about what to expect, why, and how to deal with your own feelings.

This year as in past years, the seminars were held in room 213. The program ran from Monday, March 13 through Friday, March 17. There had been some problem with scheduling the talks because of the bad weather this winter.

Many guest speakers added to the regular representatives' presentations. The guests included several people who had been alcoholics, or who had lived with parents who are or were alcoholics. These people were candid about their home lives, and they were very happy to answer any questions asked of them.

Other guests were: Officer Lynch, from the New Canaan Police Department, who spoke about You and the Law Concerning Alcohol; Dr. Griffin, who spoke about the physical effects of alcohol; and

Please turn to Page 2

**By Gretchen Meyer**

The adventures of New York City, the chance to meet new friends, and the opportunity to exchange ideas and learn new ways to improve the school newspaper were all different aspects of the field trip to Columbia University, in which six members of the *Courant* staff and their advisor, Mrs. Mary Smith, took part. This was a national conference held by the Columbia Scholastic Press Association (CSPA) for high school journalists. The editors and reporters who participated were: Dennis Boyd, Karen Helle, Lindsay McNulty, Gretchen Meyer, Beth Mitchell and Erica Stuart.

The conference was held over three days, March 16-18, with a luncheon at the Statler Hilton Hotel culminating the occasion. 'Instead of commuting into New York, the participants stayed at the Piccadilly Hotel on 45th Street West of Broadway. The hotel was ideally located, in the middle of the theatre district and a block away from the subway which was used for almost all transportation. New York City was an experience in itself, and of course being there on a holiday weekend (St. Patrick's Day) only added to the festivities of the *Courant* Staff.

Not only did the editors and reporters have fun but they also learned a great deal. Everyone took advantage of the many sectional seminars such as layout and graphics demonstrations, lectures on the principles of journalism, writing clinics and roundtable discussions with other high school journalists. Trading school newspapers and problems was a sight often seen and heard.

The journalism conference was a total success in the eyes of the participants and their advisor. The *Courant* staff has returned from a weekend filled with memories, friendships and a great deal of knowledge!!

## THE RUSSIANS ARE COMING!!!!

**By Nicole Meyer**

Approximately 50 Youth For Understanding students living in Connecticut, their host brothers and sisters, and local host families, spent an enjoyable weekend in New Canaan and Darien during an International Weekend.

Youth For Understanding is a non-profit organization which sends American and foreign students abroad yearly. As many as 6,000 students enjoy a summer or year in the foreign country of their choice. Anyone age 14 through 18 may participate in the program and live with a host family in one of 23 countries in Europe, Latin America, the Far East, or Australia.

The students arrived at the Stamford train station on Saturday afternoon, April 1. It was an unforgettable experience looking for host families and foreign students amid the hordes of people. The students were involved in a variety of activities such as a pot-luck supper on Saturday night and an ethnic trip into New York City on Sunday. Some attractions were The Statue of Liberty, Chinatown, Little Italy, sections of Eastern Europe and Russia, ending the day in Greenwich Village.

On Monday, the foreign students and "returnees" spent the day at Darien High School culminating International Week. The students spoke to various classes about their precious experiences abroad. Monday night was a sad time while new friendships were meant to remember as the students boarded the train to return home.

## LOOK OUT!

**By Karen Helle**

Just as little kids impatiently await Christmas for a glimpse of Santa, or others — Thanksgiving for turkey, so do the pranksters of the world wait for April Fool's Day. According to the custom, April 1st is designated an Anything Goes Day which ends up being a battle of the clever versus the gullible. The idea of the day is to trick as many people as possible without getting bitten yourself.

Tricks range from the all-time favorites, like switching the sugar and the salt and putting a frog in the desk, or crackers in a short-sheeted bed, to mechanical, marketable gags such as the squirting boutonniere or the handshake buzzer, to some so bizarre that they are quite unmentionable.

If your home seems like a high risk area with your family plotting against you, just think about the teachers. Teachers live in fear of this day all year long. With large numbers of unpredictable students, they never know what they are going to be up against. Some of the traditional, not to be missed jokes include putting chalk in the eraser, turning all the desks around or having the entire class leave at once.

Some of the real clinchers include taping the spray nozzle in the kitchen sink, rigging doors with buckets of water, filling a car with balloons or switching the tooth paste with the hair cream. Whether you are the cunning prankster or the unfortunate victim caution should be taken. One of these days the tables will turn. If you didn't get hit this year, look out for next year!

## SCHOOL STORE

**By Nicole Meyer**

The Junior Class has recently taken over the school store, newly named Rams Supplies by Co-Managers Susan Evans and Nicole Meyer. The school store is open every day before school from 7:30 to 8:00 and during lunch periods. For those of you who do not know where Rams Supplies is located, just look at the showcase outside the South Lounge and follow the colored arrow (just next door to the elevator.)

The music you hear during lunch is operated from the school store and run by Bill Merikallio and Sean Riley for your listening pleasure. Rams Supplies carries all the school items you need for a hard day's work, such as pencils, pens, paper and notebooks.

Compared with discount stores, the school store's prices are the lowest, and their help is the friendliest! Rams Supplies will prove to be the hottest thing on campus, so come on down and be the next customer of Rams Supplies, and be proud to say in a year that you were one of its first customers!!!!!

On April 4th the New Canaan High School and Darien High School orchestras met at New Canaan for a joint rehearsal and mini-concert performed by invitation for administration, teachers and students. The selections played included Bouree in G Minor by J. S. Bach, The Russian Sailor's Dance, and highlights from West Side Story and Oliver.

Many orchestra members play more than one instrument and also participate in the NCHS marching band, concert band, wind ensemble, Norwalk Youth Symphony, Connecticut All-State Orchestra and jazz rock groups.

The student musicians and their instruments include: Janet Roorbach and Kathy Smith, piano and violin; Christine Parra and Jim Kormendi, piano; Cindy Kuhn, organ and bells; Heather Crawford, Thera Speigel, Alexandra Hurwitz, Liz Baker, Joan Bartow, Jeanine Lovejoy, Michele Vitti, Roshanna Cooper and George Godlin, violin; Adam Fischer, violin and folk guitar.

Jillian Fenton, flute and piano; Bob Morrow, flute and bassoon; Linda Krenicki, oboe, clarinet, piano and folk guitar; Tom McGovern, Ian Challis and Karen Wagner, percussion; Bruce Prescott, trumpet; Steve Pratt, trombone; Tom Paulin, viola; Alison Reilly, cello and saxophone; Meg McCaughey, flute; John LaPoint, clarinet and folk guitar; and John Rogers, cello, string bass and bass guitar.

---

*An experiment in rubber-stamp newspaper design from New Canaan High School's Publishing Workshop, Spring 1978 (taught by . . . surprise . . . Lowry Thompson).*

# EDITORIALS

## SCHOOL SPIRIT SWALLOWED BY SENIOR SLUMP

By Marcy Nichols

### FEAR OF SELF-EJECTION

This letter is written in reply to "A Seasoned Athlete."

In your Editorial, you stated many valid reasons for exempting athletes from the high school's gym requirement. These same points have been debated at coalition meetings since the beginning of this year, and several coalition members have spoken with the administration to find out why these exemptions cannot be made.

The basic reason given is that when a student chooses to go out for a team, he is agreeing to meet the demands of his sport in addition to fulfilling his academic requirements. In the same way, writers for the Courant should not be exempted from English classes, and members of the math team must take math classes.

The administration feels strongly about retaining the gym program in its present form, but if you really feel the need for a change, don't give up. Analyze the pros and cons of the issue and follow through with a specific proposal. There are plenty of other people at New Canaan High School who feel the same way you do.

Robyn Ashton
Communications Representative
Student Coalition

## SNOW DAYS

By Elizabeth Jex

## DANGER CONT....

Mr. Smith, who is the Senior Alcoholic Counselor at Norwalk Hospital.

## INSENSITIVITY ABOUNDS!

By David Eagle

---

# TELL US HOW YOU FEEL ABOUT COURANT...

## DEAR EDITOR, SCHMUCK

OH DEAR, OH DEAR, ME, HEART, NONE OF THE ABOVE

PICK ONE

### PICK MORE!!

☐ IT'S KOSHER
☐ OBSCURE
☐ Hotter'n a 4-Alarm Fire!!

☐ LOOKS TERRIFIC!!!
☐ Rubbish
☐ I CAN'T TAKE IT I'M LEAVIN TOWN
☐ WHAT ARE YOU GUYS ON?????

AND FURTHER MORE:

Signed _____

---

# FEATURES

## HAREN KELLY PRESENTS

By Haren Kelley

★ GARDY LOU ★

By Karen Helle

## CLIQUE WARFARE CAUSES CHAOS AT NEW CANAAN!!

By Monroe Trout And Michael Stone

---

# SPORTS

## GIRLS TRACK

By Leslie Dustan

## BOY'S OUTDOOR TRACK

## GIRL'S LACROSSE

By Virginia Davlin

## BOY'S TENNIS

By Paul Crispi

## ★ VARSITY LACROSSE ★

By Kristen Fredericksen

# REBUSES

A truly maddening way to play with rubber stamps is to use them in the creation of a sort of visual pun called a "rebus." Strictly speaking, a rebus is the pictorial representation of the sound of a word or a syllable of a word. It's a kind of phonetic game playing.

The early history of rebuses lies in Egyptian hieroglyphics and ancient Chinese calligraphy. Periodically the rebus enjoys a revival. In the seventeenth century, the French found them an amusing diversion; the English went through a phase of using rebuses on tavern signs; and even Benjamin Franklin is said to have given advice via a rebus.

Two books which might give you ideas for rebuses are *Mother (Goose) in Hieroglyphicks* (Dover Publications) and *A Picture Puzzle Activity Book* (Grosset & Dunlap). Each costs around a dollar. Red Rubber Valley in California makes two rubber-stamp rebus sets.

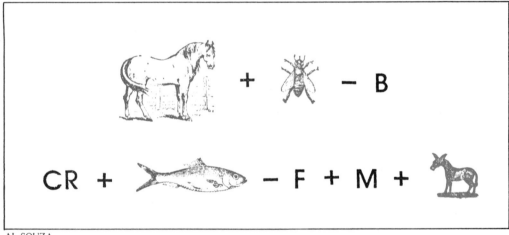

AL SOUZA

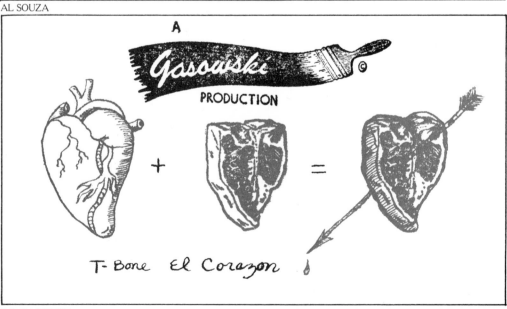

R.E. GASOWSKI

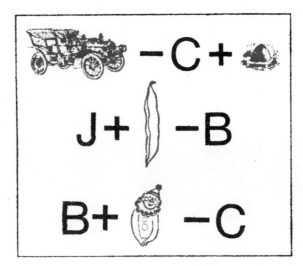

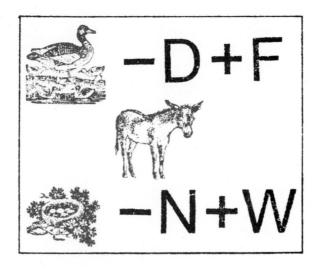

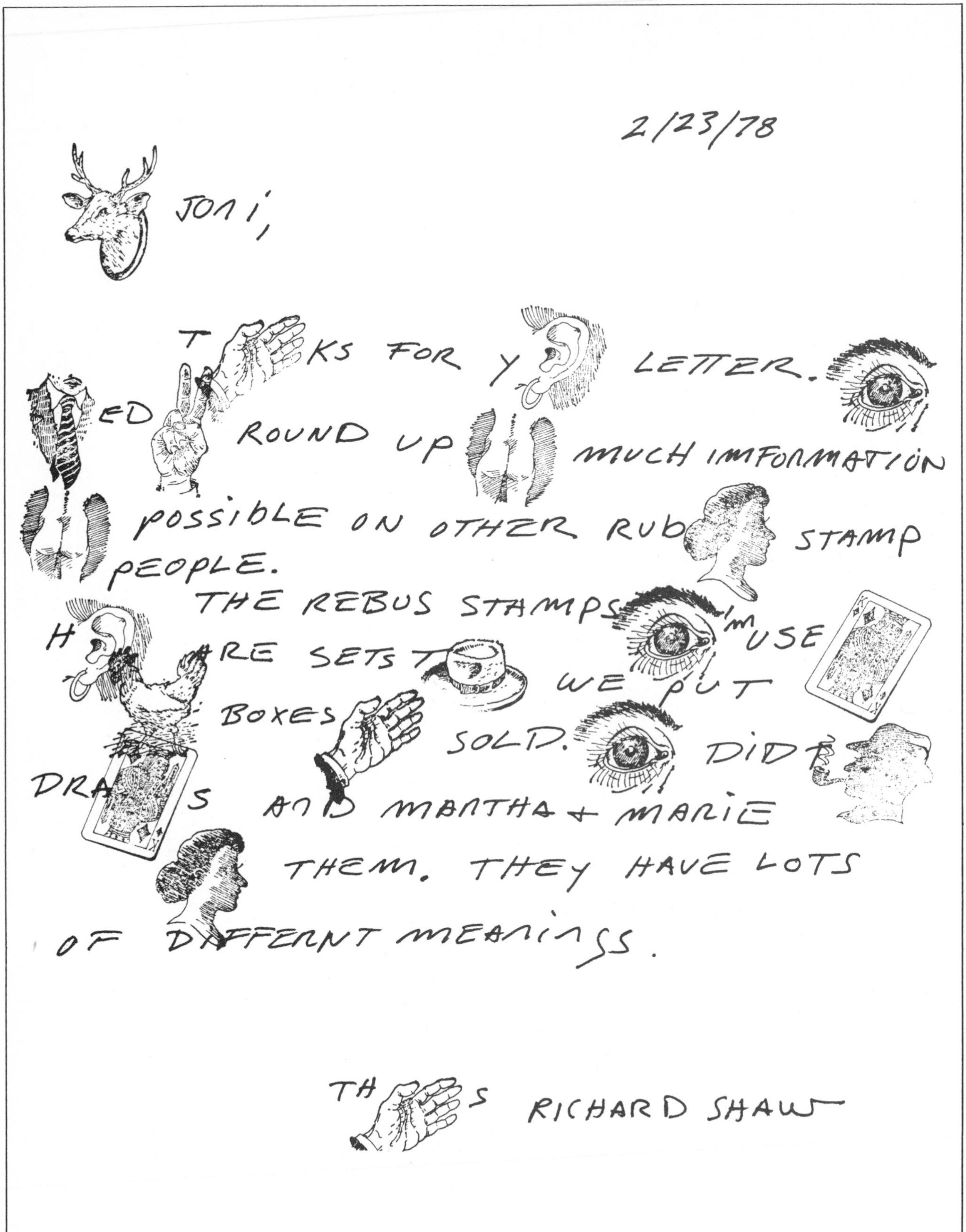

2/23/78

Joni;

T___KS FOR Y___ LETTER.

ED ___ ROUND UP ___ MUCH IMFORMATION ___ POSSIBLE ON OTHER RUB___ STAMP PEOPLE.

THE REBUS STAMPS ___ I'M USE ___ RE SETS ___ WE PUT ___ BOXES ___ SOLD. DID ___ H___ DRA___S AND MARTHA + MARIE ___ THEM. THEY HAVE LOTS OF DIFFERNT MEANINGS.

TH___S RICHARD SHAW

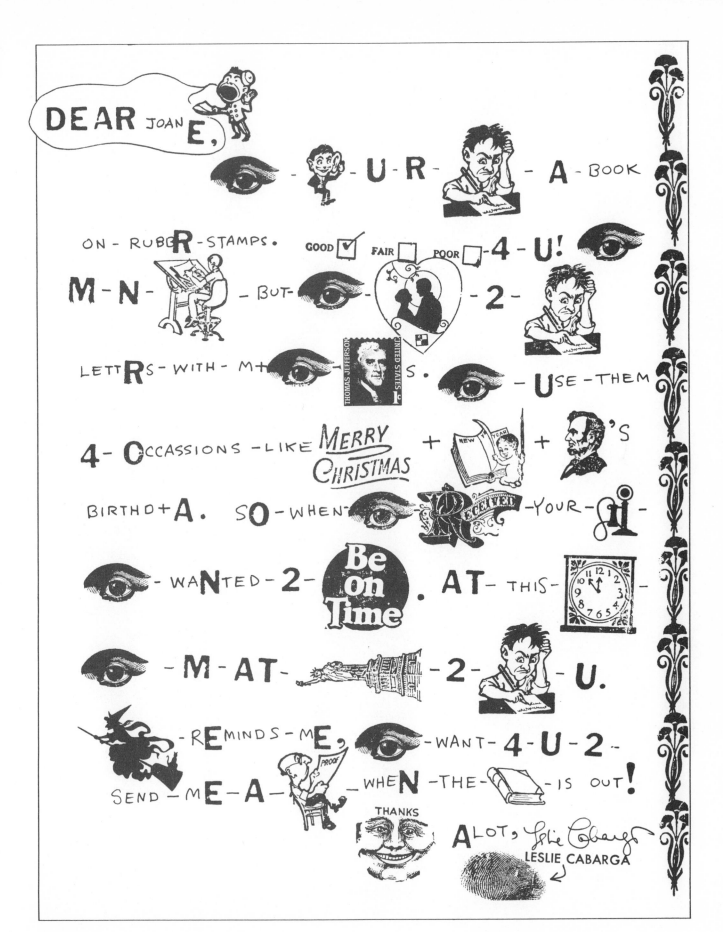

# STAMPABLE EDIBLES

At a certain point in stamp consciousness, merely stamping paper becomes old hat and you'll suspiciously start eyeing other likely surfaces with a wild gleam in your eye. When this critical beyond-paper milestone is reached, turn to the larder for inspiration. The food will appear dull and washed out. It will look, shall we say, unfinished. The tantalizingly smooth surfaces of cheeses will scream "bland, bland," eggs will look immodestly naked, and hot dogs will seem to be missing their zippers.

Before the leap into the refrigerator, one special item is required—special food ink. Basically, food inks are the same U.S. government-approved vegetable dyes that are seen indicating the grades and inspections on meat in grocery stores and meat markets. Traditionally the government stamp of approval is made with purple ink but there are other interesting colors available. The dyes, which are a hundred percent edible and water soluble, come in red, green, blue, and black in addition to purple. Edible inks are a good ace in the hole to give children with their stamps. They are safe and licking stamp pads, etc. won't pose problems. The inks can be washed out of things so if a child decides to do a number on a T-shirt or goes bonkers on the walls the world doesn't have to end. Food inks are available from commercial rubber-stamp companies or they can be ordered in one-ounce plastic bottles with a dispenser cap from Bizzaro for around $1.25 per bottle. Since demand for edible inks outside of the meat-packing industry is not overwhelming, many commercial stamp companies will probably have to special-order the ink for you. When ordering, don't forget to get an uninked foam pad for each color you plan to use.

Any rubber stamp will do for stamping food, but allowances must be made for the texture of the food to be stamped. A highly detailed stamp with a rocking chair won't look like much on the pebbled surface of an orange, for instance. The smoother the food surface, the more apt it is to take a clear impression of an image with a lot of detail. Cheese and smooth specialty meats like hot dogs and bologna are ideal. Bizzaro, whose instincts are always in the right place, has created six stamps, around $2.50 each, designed specifically for use on food.

Stamping food is not exactly a new concept, although what we're talking about here is a far cry from the more industrial food-stamping that used to go on. When trademarks hit the scene, one of the first products to bear a trademark was the Calavo brand of California avocado. At first each avocado was hand-stamped, but the process was judged too time-consuming and difficult. This is not difficult to understand. Can you imagine what it must have been like standing there at an assembly line with a stamp poised watching 240

avocados a minute whip by on a conveyor belt? The avocado people eventually switched to affixing the rubber stamps on the spokes of a rimless wheel which was then "walked over" the avocados. Stamping also figured in the citrus industry. After oranges, lemons, and grapefruit had gone through the whole routine of getting washed, oiled, shined, inspected, graded, and sorted, they were passed under rubber belts that stamped Sunkist or whatever on their surfaces. For decades eggs were carefully marked with their grade or the farmer's name by gently tapping them with special stamps. The same funny little stamps used on eggs were also well suited to stamping brand names on golf balls.

And of course there is the tale, presumably a true one, that appeared in the June 1909 issue of *Stamp Trade News* under the headline RUBBER STAMP FRITTERS. It seems the wife of a Washington stamp man served a large rubber-stamp fritter to her husband one night for dessert. Closely watched by amused friends, the husband manfully struggled to cut his fritter until the awful truth dawned on him. It was the wife's not-so-subtle way of letting her husband know she was tired of hearing nothing but rubber-stamp talk at home.

# DEFAMATION OF CHARACTER

Sublimating the urge for a tattoo because you've been unwilling to make a total commitment of the flesh? Satisfy the urge and still maintain the natural state of your own hide by turning your rubber stamp on yourself. Stamps can transform the body into a living work of art. The best designs to choose are those with a little action going on like leaping fish or shooting stars. Hearts make good beauty marks and a skull and crossbones could go anywhere. Use edible ink, the same kind used to stamp food. It is safe, nontoxic, and will wash off with soap and water.

Stamping yourself is only slightly more complex than stamping an orange or a lemon. Adjust your touch to the softer, more pliable feeling of skin and try to avoid stamping areas that are wrinkled (heaven forbid) or parts of the body that bend.

All body stamping is not necessarily narcissistic. In 1928, U.S. Marines supervising elections in Nicaragua found they could crimp the style of provincial politicos who were in the habit of recycling voters through the polls for a few extra votes. They stamped each voter's hand after he cast his ballot.

Zillions of people have had their hands stamped at dances, bars, discos, fairs, race tracks, amusement parks, etc. Some places use invisible ink. If would-be gate-crashers plague your wide-scale entertainment plans and a forty dollar investment doesn't scare you off, drop a line to the Stroblite Company, Incorporated, 10 East Twenty-third Street, New York, New York 10010, and ask for their free brochure. In it you'll find a line of Stroblite Invisible Identifier Kits (a pint of invisible ink, a stamp pad, a stamp that says PASS and an ultraviolet blacklight lamp).

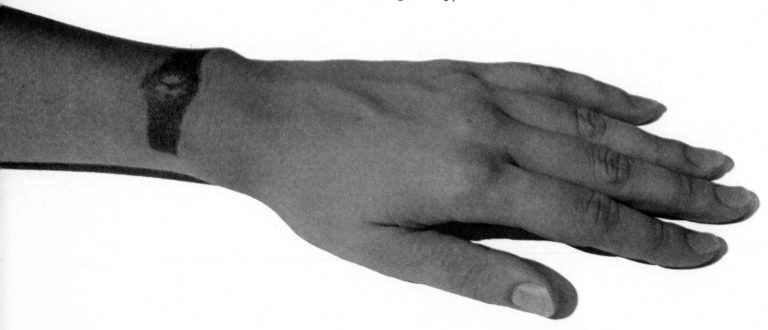

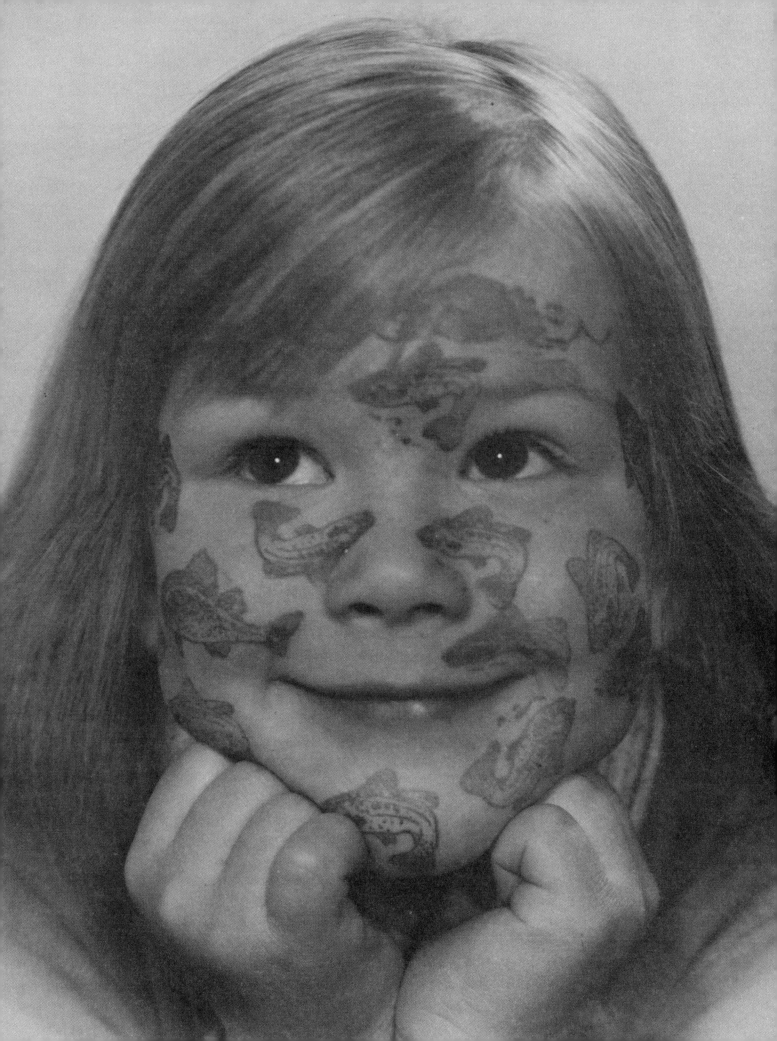

# THE POST-MASTER GENERAL'S COLLECTION

There can be little doubt in anyone's mind that the U.S. Postal Service is hooked on rubber stamps. Strictly speaking, they may well have the world's largest collection.

In 1938, *Marking Devices* magazine came right out and asked how many the Service had. S.W. Purdum, Fourth Assistant Postmaster General, responded, "Please be advised that the Department does not have readily available information covering the number of ordinary rubber stamps used annually throughout the Postal Service. However, during the past fiscal year, ending June 30, a total of 169,778 ordinary rubber stamps were purchased." It is clear Mr. Purdum had never seen an extraordinary rubber stamp.

SPECIAL HANDLING

UNDELIVERABLE AS ADDRESSED

PLEASE ADVISE CORRESPONDENTS OF YOUR CORRECT MAILING ADDRESS

Insufficient address

Please Note: this is not your correct mailing address. Notify sender to correct it.

NEW CANAAN, CT. 06840

RETURNED FOR POSTAGE

SECOND CLASS

NEWSPAPERS

PERISHABLE

GIFT NO EXPORT LICENSE REQUIRED

RETURN RECEIPT REQUESTED

SPECIAL HANDLING

RESTRICTED DELIVERY

DAMAGED IN HANDLING IN THE POSTAL SERVICE

Found in supposed empty equipment

SAM

PAL

DAMAGED IN HANDLING IN THE POSTAL SERVICE

NEW CANAAN, CT. 06840

# NOT ISSUED

**RETURN RECEIPT REQUESTED**

Return Receipt Requested
Showing Address
Where Delivered

APR 0 8 1978

## SPECIAL DELIVERY

# THIRD CLASS

RETURNED TO SENDER

## PRIORITY NAIL

REASON CHECKED
Unclaimed_____ Refused____
Addressee unknown _____
Insufficient Address _____
No such street____ number____
No such office in state____
Do not remail in this envelope

## SPECIAL DELIVERY

MISDIRECTED

## DELIVER TO ADDRESSEE ONLY

# FRAGILE

Received Unsealed at

**FORWARDING ADDRESS EXPIRED**
ROUTE NO.       INITIALS

Ask your post office or carrier for
the form for notifying others of
your correct address.

## SPECIAL 4th CL. RATE

SPECIAL FOURTH CLASS RATE
☐ ....................
☐ BOOKS
☐ MANUSCRIPT
☐ SOUND RECORDINGS
☐ 16 MILLIMETER FILMS

NAME
1st Notice_____
2nd Notice_____
Return_____

REGISTERED

NO.

UNDELIVERABLE AS ADDRESSED

Received in bad condition at

POSTAGE DUE_____ ¢
Forwarding postage guaranteed
by addressee.

# FRAGILE

# INSPECTED

NEW CANAAN, CONN.
8:30 AM TO 5 PM DAILY
10:00 AM TO 12 NOON SAT

RETURNED TO SENDER

AIR MAIL
SPECIAL DELIVERY

## REGISTERED NO.

Postage Due_____ ¢

# AIR MAIL

INSURED VALUE
$_____(U.S.)
_____DOLLARS AND_____ CENTS
_____GOLD FRANCS

LEE M. ZANDRI
FORMAN OF MAILS
NEW CANAAN, CT. 06840

SMALL PACKET

## DOO-DA POSTAGE WORKS

New York artist E.F. Higgins III has been fooling around with mail for years, and rubber-stamp imagery figures extensively in his shenanigans. He has actually worked in a rubber-stamp company in Colorado and used these skills at one point to create his own rubber-stamp catalog called *Doo-Da Art Stamps*, now defunct, which offered a strange melange of stamps. The most interesting offerings were a series of old postage cancellations turned into stamps, including a really divine one from the U.S. Postal Agency in Siberia in 1918. Higgins won second prize in the Third First International Rubber Stamp Art Exhibition.

He is involved in a wide range of instant media artforms—

Xerox art, mail art, and his current passion, postage stamps (called Doo-Da), which he makes himself. Much of the artwork for these is rubber-stamped. The designs are color-Xeroxed on gummed paper and perforated with a manual perforator that competes for space with furniture in his living room.

Higgins' personal collection shown here is wide ranging and includes eraser stamps he carved as a child, collaged stamps he made from scraps of rejected stamp dies, a set of zealous "Workers of the World" from China, and one stamp, also Chinese, that is rumored to say THE PEOPLE'S REPUBLIC OF CHINA, BUREAU OF ARTS AND CULTURE, PASSED, OK'ED.

# CACHETS

We'd never heard of a cachet until one day at an antique-paper show in Providence, Rhode Island, we wandered over to a table covered with shoe boxes. The boxes were filled with envelopes, each bearing a canceled postage stamp and a design on the lower left of the envelope. Not being involved with postal collecting, we casually flipped through a box. The designs were rather elaborate. Some looked as if they had been rubber-stamped. Rubber-stamped? Our interest quickened. We held several envelopes up to our nose for closer observation. We ran our fingers over the designs for telltale evidence that they had been printed. Some of the designs had been rubber-stamped!

We quickly bought a bunch of the envelopes and dashed across the room to show our friends Kenny and Pumpkin Speiser this monumental discovery. Kenny, glancing at our treasures, casually said, "Oh, I see you got some cachets." That was our introduction to the strange world of postal cachets.

A cachet can be printed or rubber-stamped, and usually appears on the bottom left of an envelope or postcard. Often, but not always, the design or slogan has some relationship to the postage stamp affixed to the envelope. For philatelists, the cachet alone is of little value. It is the combination of the cachet and the canceled postage stamp that grabs them.

Cachets often honor a postal event such as the first flight on an airmail route or something as simple as a national holiday like Mother's Day or Thanksgiving. Samplings from those shoe boxes are shown on the following pages.

Two places to go for more information about nonspecialty cachets are *Linn's Stamp News,* a weekly devoted to philately, and *First Days: Journal of the American First Day Cover Society* ©, specializing in cachets and first day covers. Read a few issues and then try going to some postal collecting shows. The magazines will rarely specify if a cachet is rubber-stamped or not, since that is of no interest to them. An interesting, heavily illustrated, two volume set called *Planty's Photo Encyclopedia of Cacheted FDCs,* by Dr. Earl Planty and Mike Mellone, was recently published. Each volume is $8.95 postpaid from the publisher at P.O. Box 206, Stewartsville, New Jersey 08886. Planty's book does mention rubber-stamped cachets.

Entranced by cachets, we decided to find out more, only to discover a major Naval cachet-collector in our own backyard—Frank M. Hoak III. It seems that most ships, particularly those of the Navy, have small postal departments "on board." These are the responsibility of the ships'

postal clerks. Outgoing mail is hand-canceled and a cachet is invariably added as an extra touch. The ships are proud of the designs and great thought and care go into each.

Those designed to commemorate maiden voyages or shakedown cruises are very interesting. Wording is added to the cachet to indicate which part of the voyage the ship is on at the time a letter is mailed. The fascinating naval cachets shown here are from Mr. Hoak's collection.

*Naval cachets.*

*Miscellaneous cachets.*

# STAMP OUT CHRISTMAS

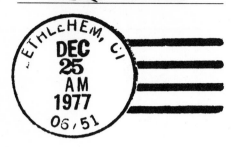

Thousands stamp out Christmas each year in tiny Bethlehem, Connecticut, a picturesque community tucked away in the rolling Litchfield Hills. In 1938, Postmaster Earl S. Johnson decided to do something about making his own Christmas mail more festive and designed a rubber stamp of a Christmas tree with the inscription MERRY CHRISTMAS FROM THE LITTLE TOWN OF BETHLEHEM. In postal-history collecting circles, such a design stamped on an envelope is called a cachet. Johnson's Christmas cachet became a Bethlehem tradition, and the post office has offered a new design each year since 1938. In the beginning, Johnson himself underwrote the cost of having the rubber stamp made each year, but the financial honors have since been assumed by the United States Postal Service.

You can't actually buy the rubber stamps, but the impressions are free. Each December the post office spreads out its collection of rubber stamps on a table in the lobby and sets out a supply of ink pads so folks can bring in their cards and packages and stamp away. Many people make the trek to Bethlehem's rubber-stamp table part of their personal Christmas tradition. Current Postmaster Jean F. Majauskas says, "Some people have been coming back for twenty-five years." One longtime visitor brings a box of candy each year as a gesture of appreciation for this unique, free service and to help keep the small staff's (three part-time clerks, three carriers) flagging energy-level up to snuff. The Bethlehem Post Office keeps special hours during the Christmas siege, even staying open on Sundays from 10:00 A.M. to 6:00 P.M. to insure that everyone gets a minute or two at the table. In some years the volume of cards, letters and packages has been as high as two hundred thousand!!!

Designs are donated by local artists, who frequently take their inspiration from the local scene. Three of the designs depict Bethlehem churches, including the one directly opposite the post office.

If you can't make the pilgrimage to Bethlehem, Connecticut, in person, there is still a way you can obtain an impression of the yearly design. Remember, this can only be done during the month of December! Write a brief note requesting an impression of the Christmas cachet. Put it in an envelope along with a self-addressed stamped envelope and mail to Postmaster, Bethlehem, Connecticut 06751. If you put a piece of heavy paper inside the self-addressed envelope, it will serve as padding, and you'll probably get a clearer impression of the cachet. The post office will stamp the Christmas cachet on your self-addressed envelope and mail it back to you.

If you really feel like getting caught up in the swing of things

*1938 cachet*

**116**

Glo ri a in excelfis
De o.
BETHLEHEM, CONN.
The
CHRISTMAS TOWN

the Christmas town
BETHLEHEM, CONN.

OLD BETHLEM MUSEUM
BETHLEHEM, CONN.

BETHLEHEM, CONN.
THE
CHRISTMAS TOWN

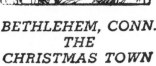

♣ CHRISTMAS TOWN
BETHLEHEM, CT.

BETHLEHEM, CONN.

"The
Christmas
Town"
Bethlehem—
Connecticut

BETHLEHEM, CONN.
THE
CHRISTMAS TOWN

"THE CHRISTMAS TOWN"

BETHLEHEM
CONNECTICUT

The Christmas
Town

BETHLEHEM
CONNECTICUT

and want the cachet to appear on all your Christmas cards, here is what you should do: Address, seal, and affix postage to each card as you normally would. Put all the cards in a box and make sure you have wrapped it sturdily for mailing. Then write a letter to the postmaster requesting the enclosed cards be stamped with the cachet and sent on their way. Don't forget that when you put a letter on the outside of a box you have to put a stamp on it, in addition to making sure the correct amount of postage is on the box.

It is worth mentioning that this whole thing is really a labor of love by the post office, so make your requests appropriate. Say "please" and "thank you" at least twelve times in your note and try to avoid sending unreasonable quantities of cards to stamp.

# MAIL ART

We can hardly discuss rubber stamps without pointing out their close association with a unique network of artistic activity that takes place through the mails called Correspondence Art (also known as Mail Art). Ask anyone involved with it for a definition and you'll hear as many definitions as there are Correspondence Artists. Our explanation is only intended to give you an inkling. Others more involved, more scholarly, have devoted entire articles to solving this definition dilemma and at this very moment a person named Michael Crane in San Diego, California is compiling the first comprehensive book on the subject..

It is generally agreed that the father of Correspondence Art is Ray Johnson, who founded the "New York Correspondence School" during the late 1950s. This was a network of "happenings" that took place through the mails, involving hundreds of artists. An interesting documentation of these goings-on was a comprehensive exhibition of the letters of Ray Johnson called Correspondence, which was held at the North Carolina Museum of Art in 1976.

Participants in the Fluxus movement were also involved in Correspondence Art around the same time, and numerous networks have followed since.

Evidence of the rubber stamp's relationship to this artform lies in the wide number of folks included in our book who either are or have been deeply involved with it . . . among them Anna Banana, Gael Bennett, Irene Dogmatic, Ken Friedman, Bill Gaglione, geORge in geORgia, Edwin "Egg" Golikov, E.F. Higgins, III, Steve Hitchcock, "Uncle Don" Milliken, the late R. Mutt, Ed Plunkett, Pauline Smith, Al Souza, Patricia Tavenner, Tinkerbelle, Endre Tot and Ben Vautier.

Correspondence Art is a form that responds to the needs of an international community of artists who do not feel art should be confined to museum or gallery walls. It reflects a highly collaborative spirit. Many pieces circulate through the mails with a suggestion by the originator that additions be made and the piece forwarded to the next person. It reflects a sense of community beyond geography, without distance or restriction, and it can be zany or frivolous or hard-hitting and political. Within the context of Correspondence Art, rubber stamps keep company with all manner of things from color Xerox and artists' postage stamps to bits of found paper ephemera and strange gummed paper labels. It is not strictly limited to letters . . . Hervé Fischer notes in his book *Art et Communication Marginale* that "among the many articles I have received from the mail, are included the following: burnt wood informing me of the German artist Klaus Groh's house fire, bits of wires which announced the installation of a telephone at the home of a Canadian artist, a sock of Ken Friedman that Fletcher Coop had painted. . ."

Correspondence Art exhibits take place continually, so if the idea intrigues you, go to it. For ourselves, we can only say that the days the post office takes a holiday are not very exciting and we always enjoy imagining what the mailman thinks when he delivers a letter sewn into a muslin sack instead of neatly placed in an envelope.

Correspondence Art is art without walls.

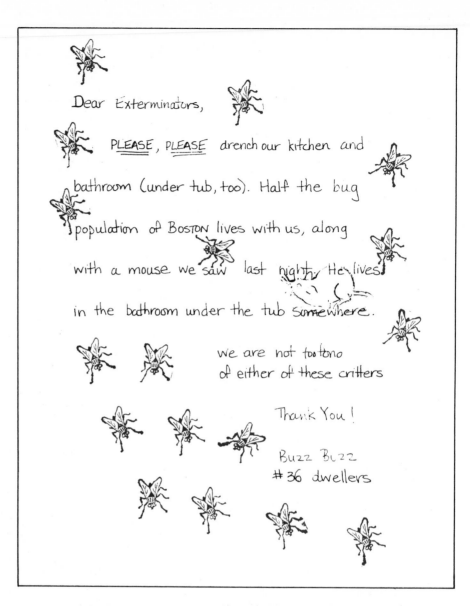

Dear Exterminators,

PLEASE, PLEASE drench our kitchen and
bathroom (under tub, too). Half the bug
population of Boston lives with us, along
with a mouse we saw last night. He lives
in the bathroom under the tub somewhere.

we are not too fono
of either of these critters

Thank You!

Buzz Buzz
#36 dwellers

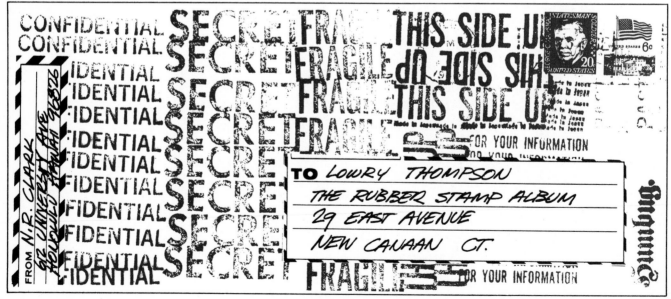

CONFIDENTIAL
CONFIDENTIAL
...IDENTIAL SECRET FRAGILE THIS SIDE UP
...FIDENTIAL SECRET FRAGILE THIS SIDE UP
FOR YOUR INFORMATION

FROM N.R. CLARK
912 UNIVERSITY AVE
HONOLULU HAWAII 96826

TO LOWRY THOMPSON
THE RUBBER STAMP ALBUM
29 EAST AVENUE
NEW CANAAN CT.

FRAGILE FOR YOUR INFORMATION

123

HOW MANY ICE CREAM CONES DO YOU THINK WE SHARED? HOW MANY TIMES DID WE DANCE? COULD WE BEGIN TO COUNT THE TIMES WE LAUGHED NONE OF THIS WILL CHANGE: BASKIN ROBBINS WILL BECOME MOTHER HALL'S ICE CREAM PARLOR; & WE WILL NEVER STOP DANCING, BUT MOST IMPORTANTLY ............ WE WILL THINK OF EACH OTHER OFTEN AND WE WILL LAUGH AND FEEL GREAT JOY – BECAUSE THAT IS WHAT YOU TAUGHT US... TO FEEL

125

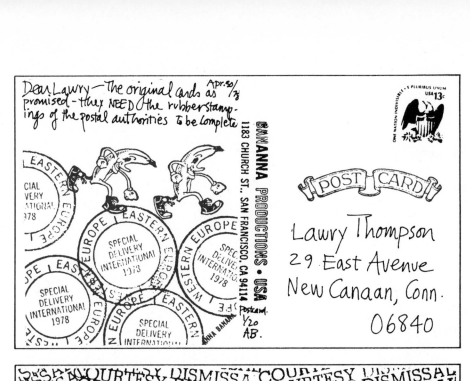

Dear Lawry—The original cards as promised—they NEED the rubberstampings of the postal authorities to be complete. Apr.50/78

BANANNA PRODUCTIONS • USA
1183 CHURCH ST., SAN FRANCISCO, CA 94114
Postcard. 1/20 AB.

POST CARD

Lawry Thompson
29 East Avenue
New Canaan, Conn.
06840

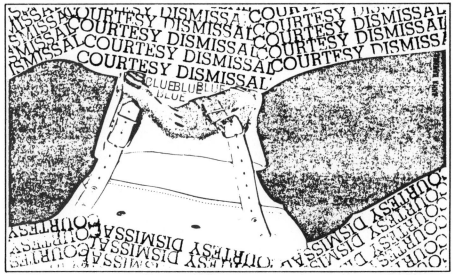

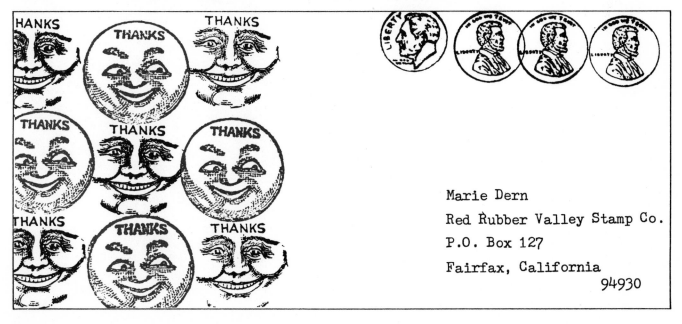

Marie Dern
Red Rubber Valley Stamp Co.
P.O. Box 127
Fairfax, California
94930

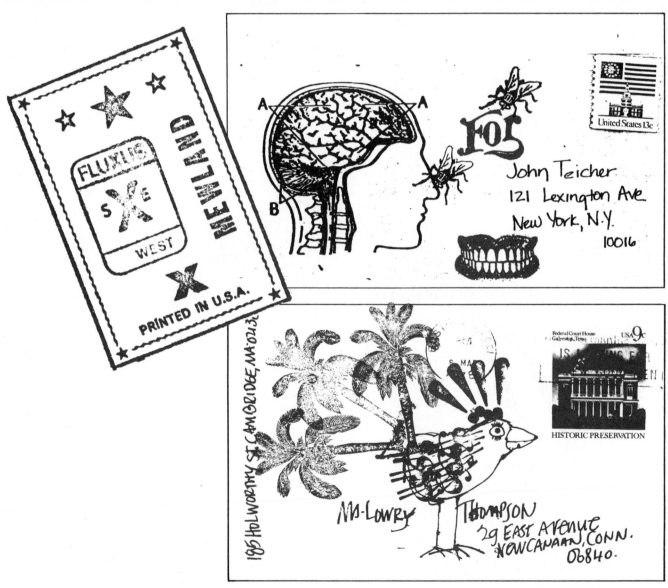

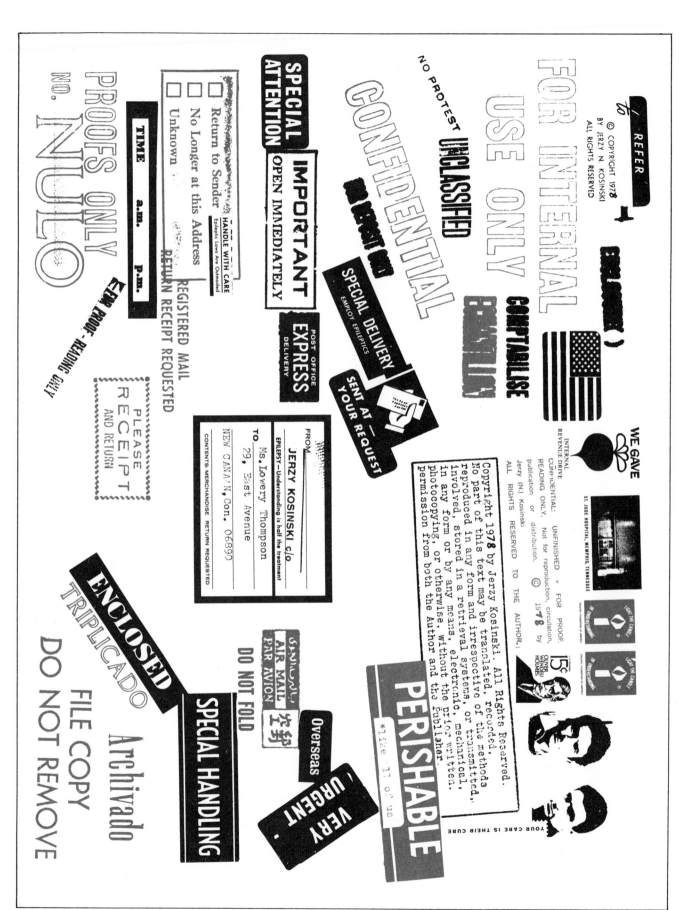

*Famed author Jerzy Kosinski designs his own rubber stamps, using them in both his work and personal correspondence. This envelope, a riot of rubber-stamping and stickers, is typical. "It drives my publishers crazy," says Kosinski.*

## Krupp Comic Works, Inc.
P.O. BOX 7 - PRINCETON, WISCONSIN 54968

VIA AIR MAIL

Nick Landau
Comic Media Dist.
10 Ladbroke Walk
London, England

AIR MAIL

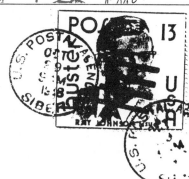

Lynn Mechanic
291 Lexington
San Francisco, CA 94110
(415) 824-5113

SAN FRANCISCO, CA 94126
PM
19 OCT
1977

Bizarro Rubber Stamp Catalogue
Box 126
Annex Station
Providence, RI 02981

FIRST OF THE RED HOT DADADS
BUSTER CLEVELAND 1943-2043

C/O DOO-DA POST
153 LUDLOW #6
N.Y.C. N.Y.
10000

ART GANGSTER

POSTAL ART

POSTAL ART

NO RUSH

LOUISE FILI

NO RUSH

"DADA SUCKS"

NO RUSH

POSTAL ART

NO RUSH

ARTIST'S LIMITED EDITION

SUITABLE FOR FRAMING

135

# dear Mr. Steinbe

## I AM PRESENTLY IN THE MIDS
## OF WRITING A BOOK ENTITLE

IT IS BEING PUBLISHED IN SEPT BY WORKMAN(K) BOOK) AND WE HOPE THE 40,000 COPIES WI BE WIDELY READ AND LOVED BY ALL. SINCE ARE TRUELY THE KING OF RUBBER STAMP THE GREATEST STAMPER IN THE LAND, I HAVE FIN OVERCOME MY FEAR OF WRITING YOU AND IT HOPE THAT YOU WILL SO THAT I MIGHT TEL MIGHT MORE ABOUT OUR PROJECT AND F HAPS SET UP A TIME TO SHOW YOU THE GREA STUFF THAT WE'VE COLLECTED FROM DA TO CORITA KENT. SO IF YOU ISSUE THE WORD THE WORD THROUGH WRITTEN OR SPOKE WORD I COULD RUN TO N.Y. AS QUICK AS A AND THEN MAYBE YOU WOULD TELL ME WHAT STARTED IT ALL FOR YOU.

I'M NOT NORMALLY SO REDUNDANT!!!

# g,

## THE RUBBER STAMP ALBUM

a book all about where to buy, how to make and the wierd and wonderful stampfreaks and their rubber stamp madness

LOWRY THOMPSON
29 EAST AVE.
NEW CANAAN, CONN.
06840

*A letter to Saul Steinberg . . . the authors received no reply.*

# MY STAMPS ARE CRAZIER THAN YOURS

ersonal logos and private collections of rubber stamps are everywhere. Many are original designs, some contain wonderful antique stamps. Most of them are pretty far removed from the sorts of stamps the first major users of rubber stamps—banks and railroads—had in their collections.

F.D.R. had a set of rubber stamps bearing the names of each of his cabinet members for use on memos, and the irrepressible Generalissimo Francisco Franco kept a collection of over one hundred rubber stamps and seals in his personal collection to make impressions on both private and public documents. His collection now resides in a government museum in Madrid.

Anything can become a personal logo. Even a simple name-and-address stamp. J.F. Walker, a member of the Louisville Chili Con Carne Club, inaugurated a new custom in 1909 by using his to sign hotel registers, much to the consternation of veteran hotel executives. One U.S. president sent out a 31,000-piece mailing, each piece carefully signed with a rubber-stamp facsimile of his signature.

Gourmet-cuisine notable Julia Child puts the finishing touch on personal correspondence with a stamp; actress Diane Keaton has a whimsical array of stamps, and writers Tom Robbins and Jerzy Kosinski have both toyed with stamps for years.

Certain designs from private collections allow their owners a certain freedom of communication that is more effective than words. One college professor with a good collection of "bull" rubber-stamps uses them to communicate briefly but thoroughly with his students when grading their papers. Some of the papers are more extensively stamped than others. F.D. Gardiner, an old-time stamp maker from Fall River, Massachusetts, used to stamp his lucky number, 9, an inch-and-a-half high on all letterheads and envelopes leaving his firm. Wonder if it helped his profits?

A clown in San Francisco reminds people of her profession on every letter; photographers leave their mark on the backs of photos with stamps; and one California illustrator found he had amazing results when he used a gigantic frog stamp to request overdue payment from his accounts.

HOMAGE TO JEAN BROWN

BILL GAGLIONE

COCK-A-DOODLE-DADDA

**MALE / MAIL ART**

GAGLIONE 1940-2040

Bill Gaglione is a jerk

PAYMENTS NOT MADE WITHIN 30 DAYS FROM INVOICE DATE ARE SUBJECT TO A SERVICE CHARGE OF 1½% PER MONTH. IF THE SERVICE CHARGE IS LESS THAN $1.00 FOR ANY MONTH, IT WILL BE COMPUTED AT $1.00.

# Dada is everywhere

30 Min. Free Parking F.W.N.B.

THIS IS A SPECIAL RUBBER STAMP ART ISSUE OF DAD(D)AZINE

NO CREDIT TAKEN

# W & W via UPS to Chicago

THE DADDALAND POSTCARD SHOW

**OK**

Made in Daddaland

THIS PAGE WAS LEFT BLANK INTENTIONALLY

BILL GAGLIONE

Figure 50.

Figure 50.—BRAIN and CORD.
1, 1, hemispheres of cerebrum; 2
great middle fissure; 3, cerebellum
4, olfactory nerves; 5, optic nerves
6, corpora albicantia; 7, motor oculi
8, pons Varolii; 9, fourth nerve; 10
medulla oblongata; 11, 11, medulla
spinalis; 12, 12, spinal nerves; 13
cauda equina.

"It's the Hair-Not the Hat"

Uneeda
GRAHAM
CRACKERS

Doigt carré

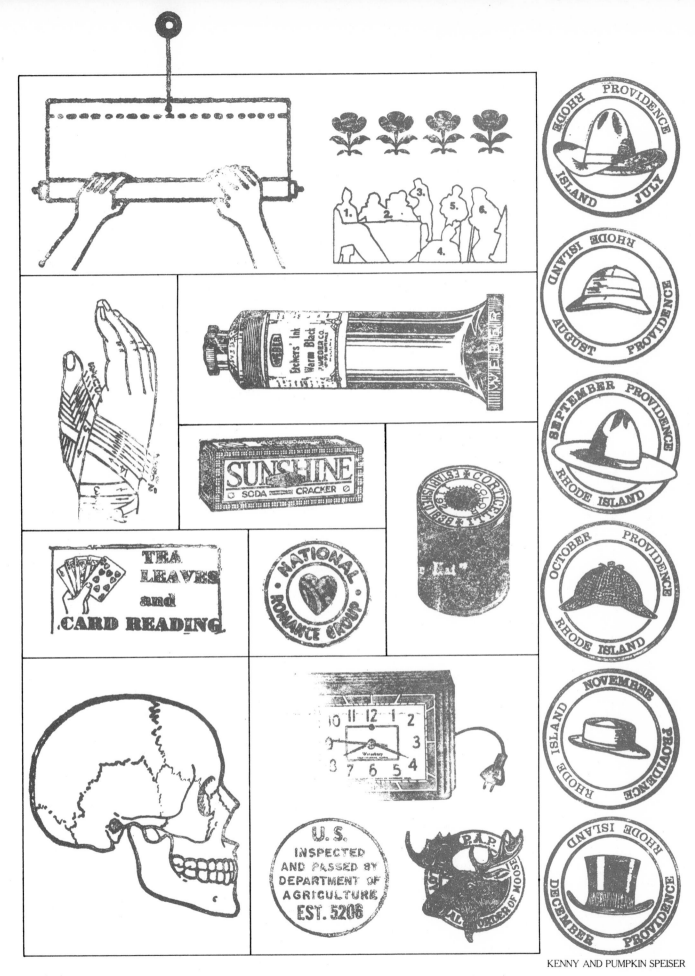

KENNY AND PUMPKIN SPEISER

141

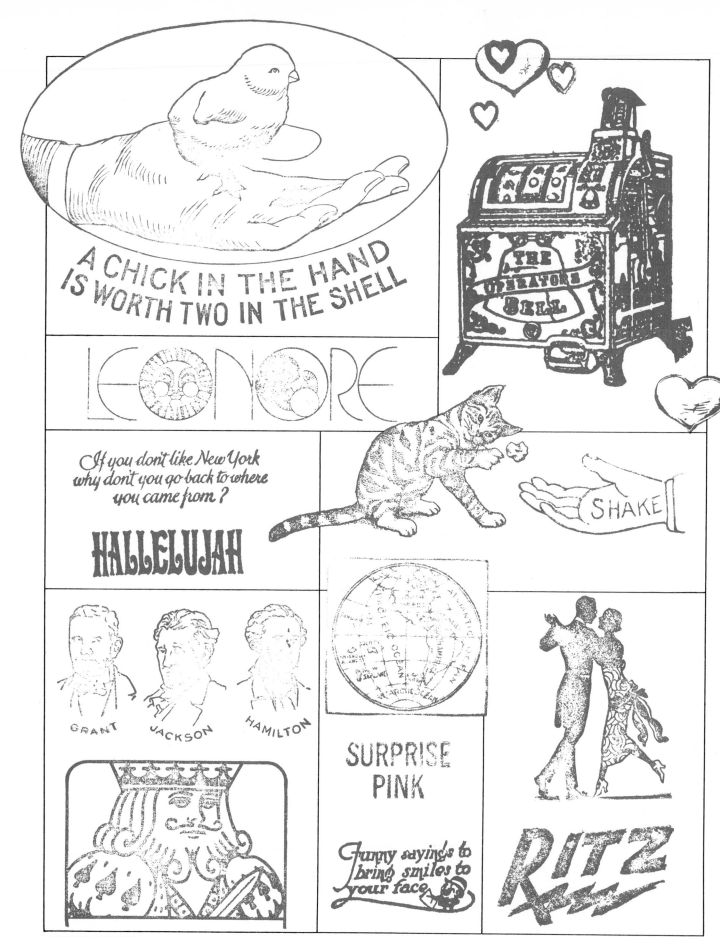

A CHICK IN THE HAND IS WORTH TWO IN THE SHELL

LEONORE

If you don't like New York why don't you go back to where you came from?

HALLELUJAH

GRANT   JACKSON   HAMILTON

SHAKE

SURPRISE PINK

Funny sayings to bring smiles to your face

RITZ

LEONORE FLEISCHER

MADE TO
STAND UP
UNDER
HARD
POUNDING
AND
CONSTANT
USE

SUZANNE S. FREEDMAN

143

*Marc David Paisin*

MARC DAVID PAISIN

BAKER'S CLAY
TERESA BLUMRICH
Albany - Oregon

STEVE BLUMRICH

NAIAD EINSEL

TERRI SULLIVAN

The Thinking Man's Tortoise is Another Man's Goat

FRS!

PETER KEVAN

SUN PRODUCTIONS · NANCY R. CLARK ·

NANCY R. CLARK

PELAVO

III
DANIEL PELAVIN

WALTER EINSEL

FOR DEPOSIT ONLY TO
GREETINGS
#0089-026736
WELLS FARGO
THANK YOU

LYN FOLEY

**DO NOT**
ABUSE, BEND, CLIP, DEFACE, ERASE, FOLD,
GOUGE, HACK, IGNORE, JUNK, KERF, LOSE,
MUTILATE, NEGLECT, OCCLUDE, PUNCTURE,
QUARTER, ROLL, SPINDLE, TAINT, UGLIFY,
VEX, WRINKLE, X-RAY, YERK OR ZAP THIS
**ARTWORK**
NIKOLAI GREGORIC III

**ACCIDENT**
*prone*

JIM BOLIN

NIKOLAI GREGORIC III

POST MARK GRAPHICS
354
PANORAMIC
WAY
549 3921

The Picture Plane By
EDGE GOLIK GOLIKOFF
I AM THE MOST,
EGG GOLIK GOLIKOV

APRES DARDAR SYSTEMS

THE WASTE IS A TERRIBLE
THING TO MIND - E.G.G. EDWIN G. GOLIKOV

AL CHING

ANNA BANANA

NANCY R. CLARK

SCULPTURE & GRAPHICS · MARY SMITH 579, POST ST. #369. SF. CA. 94109.

K. MARY SMITH

K. MARY SMITH

This certificate also bestows life membership in

# THE ROYAL ORDER OF BANANA

For details   BANANNA PRODUCTIONS · USA
Anna Banana,   1183 CHURCH ST., SAN FRANCISCO, CA 94114

ANNA BANANA

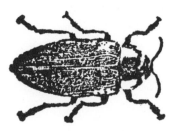

ANTHONY REVEAUX

RABID TRANSIT

IRENE DOGMATIC

KEEP SMILING

IRENE DOGMATIC

ACHTUNG!

PLEASE HAND STAMP

STAMP OUT CREATIVITY
STAMP OUT CREATIVITY
STAMP OUT CREATIVITY

ELIZABETH LIDE

KRISTI WARREN

*Anna Banana Crates of Bananas Tarzana B. Nana*

ANNA BANANA

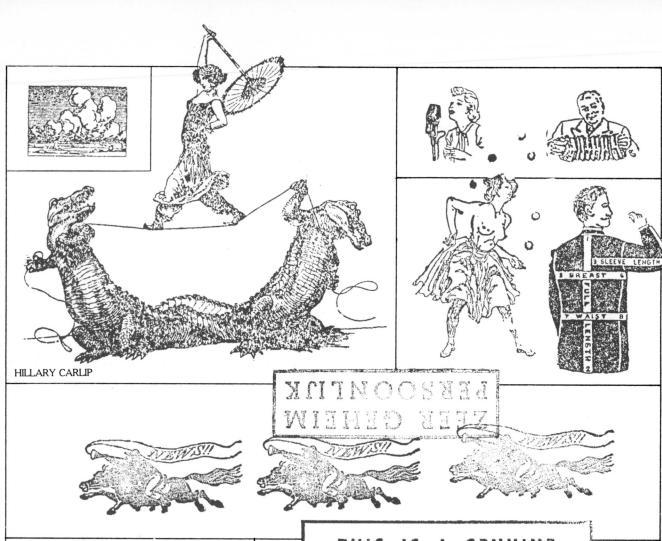

HILLARY CARLIP

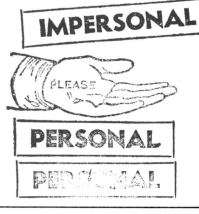

DAVID BASCOM

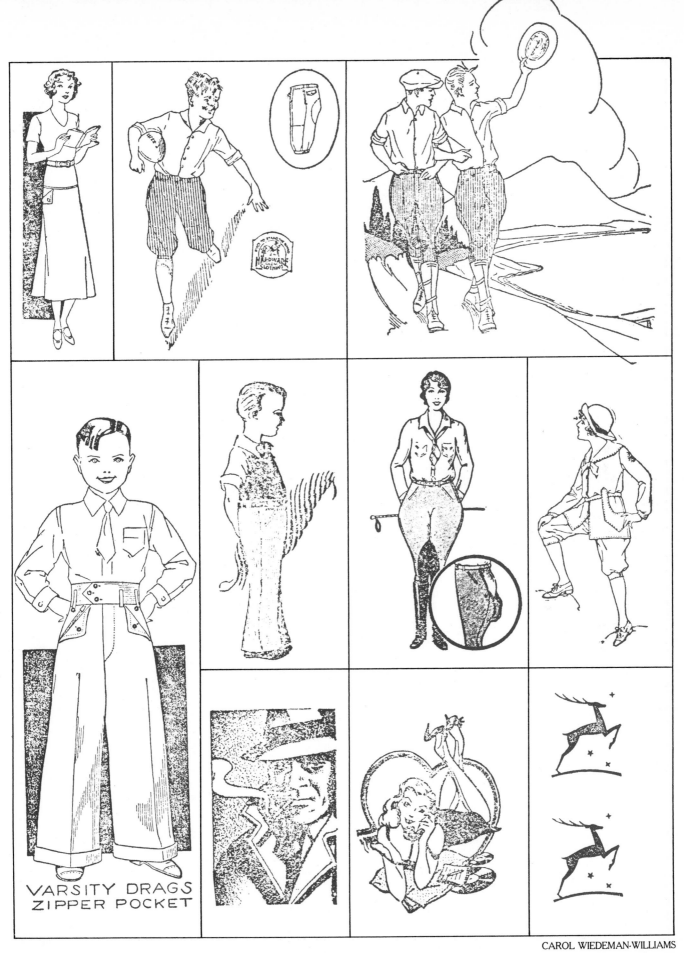

VARSITY DRAGS
ZIPPER POCKET

CAROL WIEDEMAN-WILLIAMS

**147**

MAIL CHAUVINIST

Durland, Box 805, Amherst...

STEVEN DURLAND

**AL SOUZA PHOTOWORKS**

AL SOUZA

OR OR OR OR

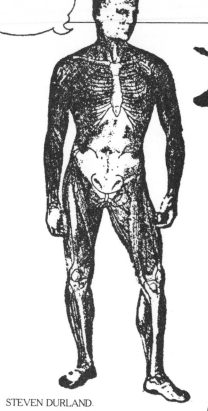

STEVEN DURLAND.

ORFICIAL

**FIRST OF FIVE POSSIBLE VERSIONS**
**SECOND OF FIVE POSSIBLE VERSIONS**
**THIRD OF FIVE POSSIBLE VERSIONS**
**FOURTH OF FIVE POSSIBLE VERSIONS**
**FIFTH OF FIVE POSSIBLE VERSIONS**

GEORGE LOVES SALLY

PAGATO
FATT. COMM. APERTA
RACCOMANDATA
VIA AEREA
STAMPE

MANOSCRITTI
COPIA
SENZA SPESE
REGISTRATO

geORge in geORgia (GEORGE H. BRETT II)

**FROM INNSBRUCK WITH LOVE**

**FROM AMHERST WITH LOVE**

*FROM PARIS WITH LOVE*

*FROM GENEVA WITH LOVE*

AL SOUZA

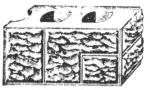

MEL R. TEARLE

**SO I SEZ —
WHO LOOKS AT
THE BOTTOMS?**
STEVEN DURLAND

YOUR
FACE

STEVEN DURLAND

148

PLEASE REPLY JOHN DOE coilage by ray johnson SILHOUETTE UNIVERSITY

SPAGHETTI CLUB
BUDDHA UNIVERSITY
SPAM BELT CLUB
BLUE EYES CLUB
MADAM RED
KOOL CLUB
BUDDHA UNIVERSHITY
OF VANCOUVER
KACHINA CLUB
ONLY UNIVERSITY
RAY JOHNSONG

EDIE BEALE FAN CLUB

COLLAGE BY RAY JOHNSON
SHELLEY DUVALL FAN CLUB
SHELLEY DUVALL FAN CLUB
COLLAGE BY TOBY SPISELMAN
TOILET PAPER
GEORGE BRECH
BUDDHA UNIVERSITY PRESS
EMILY DICKINSON UNIVERSITY
Coll
Ages
By Ray Johnson
EVAPORATIONS BY RAY JOHNSON

PALOMA PICASSO FAN CLUB

BOOTA UNIVERSITY

Cool Age  By Ray Johnson

DRIP

THIS IS NOT BUNNY

BLUE EYES CRUB

FETUS JOHNSON

DO NOT SPEAK

DEAD PAN CLUB

BLUSH

RAY JOHNSON
44 WEST 7 STREET
LOCUST VALLEY
NEW YORK 11560

RAY JOHNSON
100 COPIES
44 WEST 7 STREET
LOCUST VALLEY
NEW YORK 11560

JOHNSON CITY, TENN.

JADE

MY FUNNY VERLAINETINE
COLLAGE BY RAY JOHNSON

MY FUNNY VALENTINE
JOHN DOE 1967

MY FUNNY VALESTINE
RAY JOHNSON
Golden File Award
CONFIDENTIAL
THE PINK HOUSE
RAY JOHNSON
44 WEST 7 STREET
LOCUST VALLEY
NEW YORK 11560

My Funny Verlainetine

TALKING SILHOUETTE UNIVERSITY
TALKING SILHOUETTE UNIVERSITY
"EARLY COLLAGE BY RAY JOHNSON"
COLLAGE BY RAY JOHNSON
COLLAGE BY BILL MAULDIN
DOUGHNUT FESTIVAL
FACE COLLAGE BY RAY JOHNSON
COLLAGE BY A MAJOR ARTIST
COLLAGE BY SUZY KNICKER KNOCKERS
COLLAGE BY SUZY KNICKERBOCKERS
UBBAGE BY RAY JOHNSON
COLLAGE BY AL SOUZA
ED PLUNKETT FAN CLUB
III    LITHOGRAPH BY RAY JOHNSON
COLLAGE BY ALEXANDRA FINDLAY

EDWIN GOLIKOFF
1239 SANTA FE DRIVE N.
DENVER, COLORADO 80204
COLLAGE BY RAY JOHNSON 1973

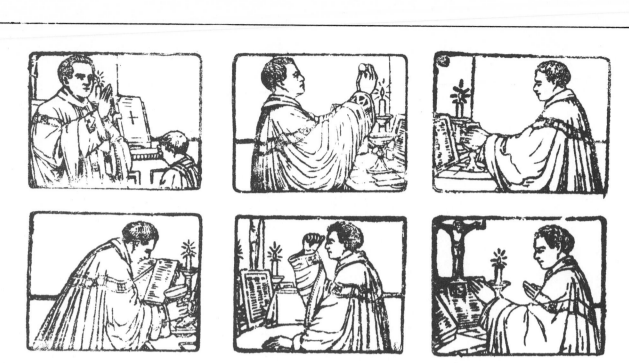

*A set of religious rubber stamps, vintage 1930, from the collection of Paul M. Levy.*

CHARLENE M. MODENA

PETER GRECO

LYN TIEFENBACHER

ENDRE TOT

PAUL M. LEVY

ENDRE TOT

DANIEL PELAVIN

STACY L. MANN

Alice McGrath

ALICE McGRATH

G.A.S.

IRVA MANDELBAUM

MICHAEL ACKER

ICE

Moons of Mar
Ballroom

E.M. PLUNKETT

LOUISE FILI

## MUST BE ENDORSED BY THE PAYEE IN PERSON, OR IF A CORPORATION, MUST BE SIGNED BY AN OFFICER GIVING HIS TITLE.

Waiver of Liens: We, the undersigned, are general or subcontractors, materialmen, or other persons furnishing services or labor or materials, in the construction or repair of improvements upon real estate described on voucher.

In consideration hereof, and other benefits accruing to us, and in order to procure the making of one or more loans on said real estate, as improved, we do hereby waive, release and quit-claim in favor of each and every party making a loan on said real estate, as improved, and his or its successors and assigns, all right that we, may now have to a lien upon the land and improvements described on the voucher which was attached to this check and bears the same number, by virtue of the laws of the State of Colorado and we do further warrant that we have not and will not assign our claims for payment, nor our right to perfect a lien against said property, and that we have the right to execute this waiver and release thereof.

We respectively warrant that all laborers employed by us upon the aforesaid premises have been fully paid and that none of such laborers have any claim, demand, or lien against said premises; and further, that no chattel mortgage, conditional bill of sale or retention of title agreement has been given or executed by the said owner or any general contractor or any party, for or in connection with any material, appliances, machinery, fixtures, or furnishings placed upon, or installed in the aforesaid premises by us.

It is understood and agreed that the signature hereto is for all services rendered, work done and material furnished heretofor by the signer in any and all capacities and is not understood to be only for any particular item. The endorsement on this check is full execution of foregoing waiver and shall be my signature thereon.

RUSTY GREEN

TOM ROBBINS

√ THE SQUARE ROOT

FLORIST, WESTPORT, CT.

1100 MADISON AVE. S.O. Saxe NEW YORK, N.Y. 10028

STEPHEN O. SAXE

A VACUUM IS NOTHING TO AVOID

ELAINE BOGDONOV GINSBERG

151

# THE RUBBER STAMP PRINCE

If the American government ever decides to follow the lead of Japan and designate certain artists "living treasures," our vote would absolutely go to elfin Barton Lidice Beneš, an extraordinary New York artist.

On our first visit to his studio we got so excited we could hardly speak. Barton was excited, too, but for different reasons. He had just received a New York State Council on the Arts grant for his rubber-stamp works.

Barton's actual stamp collection was quite small when we first met him, but the things he did with those few stamps were amazing. It seems he has this aunt, Aunt Evelyn, a recluse who lives in Florida. Twice each week she mails Barton a typewritten, fifty-page letter. The letters are somewhat stream-of-consciousness in form, cover hundreds of subjects, and reflect the sensibilities of the elderly in touching and dynamic ways. Barton has created an entire artform using Aunt Evelyn's letters as the basis for a series of limited edition, rubber-stamped works and books. In each, he stamps the text out word for word. Since Aunt Evelyn is far from terse in these letters, it becomes apparent that Barton is an individual of enormous patience.

One particularly poignant piece, called "Tears," is a set of delicate, embroidered handkerchiefs stamped with Aunt Evelyn's description of how she was unable to deal with grief, and cry after the death of her husband. The handkerchiefs are neatly piled in the same box with a clear plastic lid which they were originally purchased in. Barton has also stamped Aunt Evelyn's thoughts on "poisoned cookies" on a rolling pin.

The ultimate Beneš creations are enormous Oriental-carpet designs rubber-stamped on enormous sheets of paper. Elsewhere in the book you'll find two of these which were especially designed as Barton's gift to our book.

His works have appeared at the Fendrick Gallery in Washington, D.C., the Princeton Gallery of Fine Arts, the Center for Book Arts in New York, as well as many other galleries. His recent rubber-stamp work was the subject of a one-man show at Stempelplaats in Amsterdam.

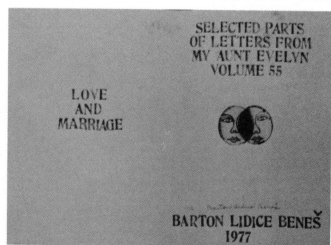

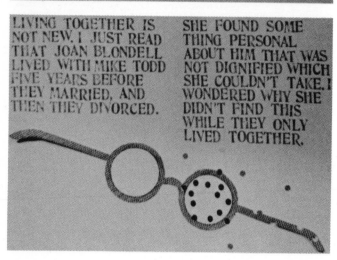

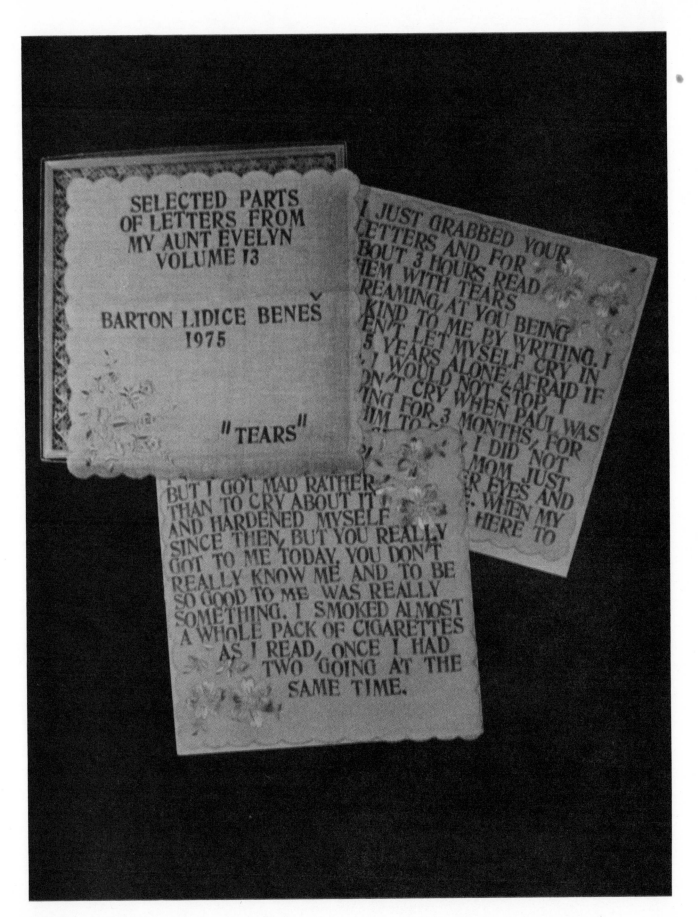

SELECTED PARTS
OF LETTERS FROM
MY AUNT EVELYN
VOLUME 13

BARTON LIDICE BENEŠ
1975

"TEARS"

I JUST GRABBED YOUR
LETTERS AND FOR
ABOUT 3 HOURS READ
THEM WITH TEARS
STREAMING AT YOU BEING
KIND TO ME BY WRITING. I
WENT LET MYSELF CRY IN
5 YEARS ALONE, AFRAID IF
I WOULD NOT STOP Y
DON'T CRY WHEN PAUL WAS
DYING FOR 3 MONTHS, FOR
HIM TO D           I DID NOT
                   MOM JUST
                ER EYES AND
              WHEN MY
             HERE TO

BUT I GOT MAD RATHER
THAN TO CRY ABOUT IT
AND HARDENED MYSELF
SINCE THEN, BUT YOU REALLY
GOT TO ME TODAY, YOU DON'T
REALLY KNOW ME AND TO BE
SO GOOD TO ME WAS REALLY
SOMETHING. I SMOKED ALMOST
A WHOLE PACK OF CIGARETTES
AS I READ, ONCE I HAD
TWO GOING AT THE
SAME TIME.

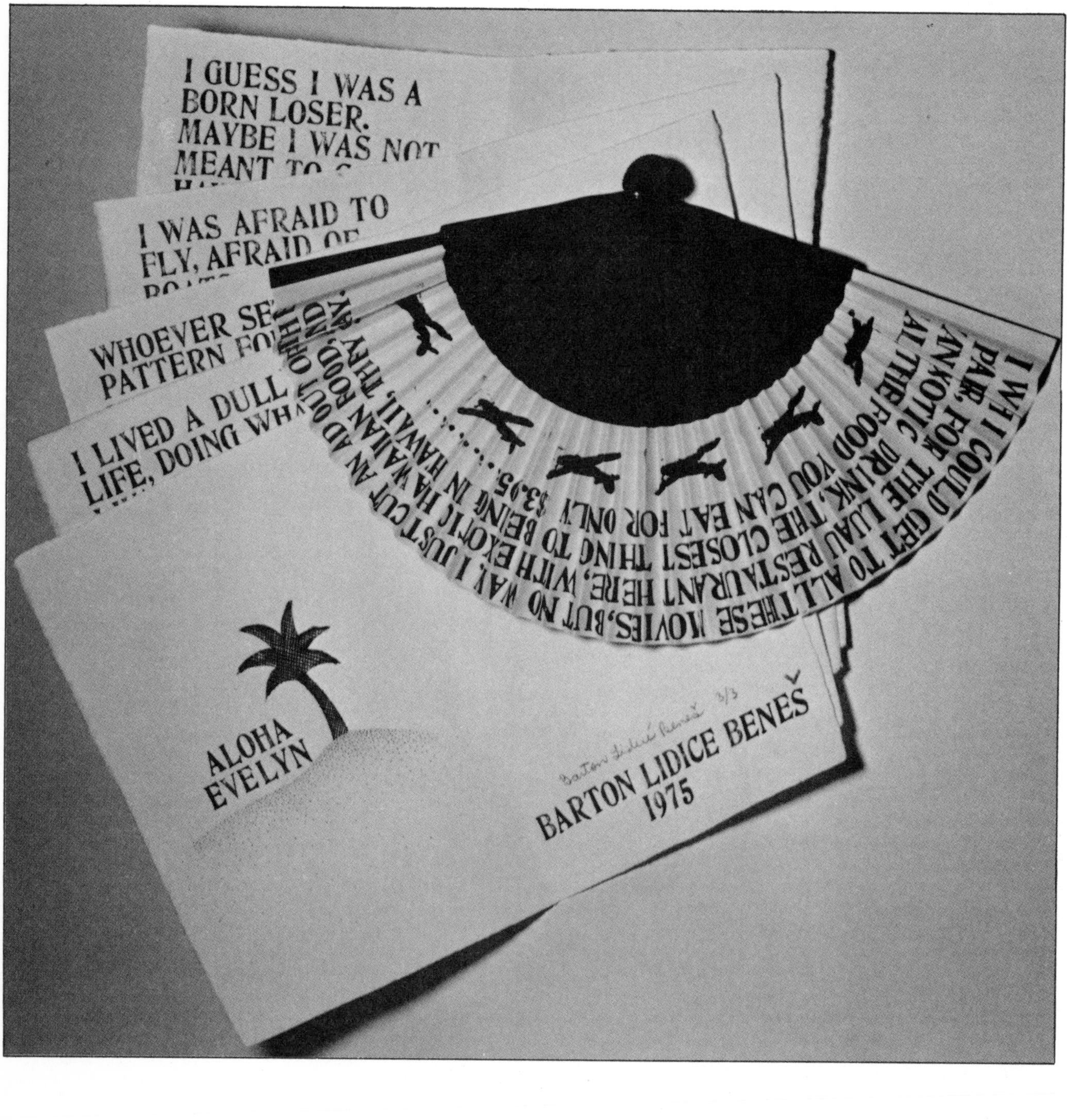


PHOTO: ANDRES LANDER

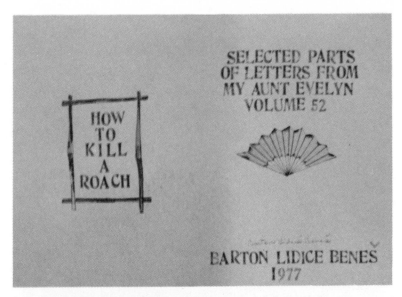

HOW
TO
KILL
A
ROACH

SELECTED PARTS
OF LETTERS FROM
MY AUNT EVELYN
VOLUME 52

BARTON LIDICE BENEŠ
1977

I DO LOOK KINDLY AT
EACH ONE BEFORE I
SQUASH HIM, I DON'T GO
INTO HYSTERICS. ON
THAT DRAINBOARD,
WHEN I PUT THE LIGHT
ON, AND MOVE SOME
THING, THEY SCOOT.
THEY FIND ONE THING
AND ALWAYS, WITHOUT
FAIL, GET BEHIND IT
ON THE OPPOSITE SIDE
FROM WHERE I AM AND
STAY PUT. I ALWAYS
WOULD GO FOR THE
SPRAY OR SWATTER,
AND NOT SEE THEM, SO
FEEL THEY GOT AWAY,

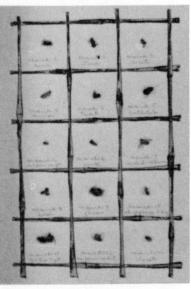

BUT NOT SO, THEY DON'T
MOVE AT ALL, THEY JUST
WAIT UNTIL I GIVE UP. SO
THE OTHER NIGHT THIS
HAPPENED, AND I SAW
WHERE IT HID, I TOOK MY
TIME GETTING THE
SWATTER. I MOVED
EVERYTHING OUT OF THE
WAY, FOR CLEAR
SWATTING, AND THEN I
WAS READY. I MOVED
THE JAR IT WAS BEHIND,
AND BLOCKED THE BACK,
SO IT HAD TO GO FOWARD
TO THE EMPTY SINK, AND
I GOT IT ON THE EDGE,
STUNNED IT, AND THEN

SWEPT IT TO THE
FLOOR WHERE I
REALLY SWATTED IT.

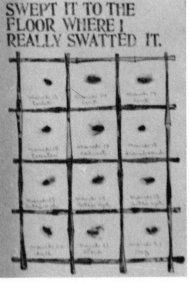

# RUBBER STAMP MADNESS

One of the first to integrate the rubber stamp in works of art was German artist/poet Kurt Schwitters, who dubbed his art activities "Merz" (from a scrap of paper with the word KOMMERZ used in one of his early collages). "Merz" applies to the bulk of Schwitter's work, not exclusively to the pieces incorporating stamps. As early as 1919 he created "Merz rubber-stamp drawings," which were an amalgam of pasted bits of paper, drawings and stamp impressions made with common, functional stamps that bore phrases such as BELEGEXEMPLAR (Review Copy) and BEZAHLT (Paid). A hefty art tome entitled *Kurt Schwitters,* written by Werner Schmalenbach (published by Harry N. Abrams, 1967), shows four examples of Schwitters' works containing rubber-stamp impressions. Probably the first book of rubber-stamp works was Schwitters' *Sturm Bilderbuch IV,* published in Berlin in 1920, which contains fifteen poems and fifteen rubber-stamp drawings.

An article in the Special Catalog Edition of La Mamelle's *Front,* written by Ken Friedman and Georg M. Gugelberger, dates the introduction of the stamp into contemporary art to Ben Vautier's use of a rubber stamp (LART CEST) in his works in 1949.

Both German artist Dieter Roth and French artist Arman began using stamps heavily in their works in the 1950s. A number of Roth's books are available from Edition Hansjorg Mayer, D7000 Stuttgart 1, Engelhornweg 17, West Germany, including a reprint edition of a 1967 literary work with stamp drawings called *Mundunculum.* This same firm also lists in their catalog a costly Roth work called *Stamp Box* which consists of twelve actual rubber stamps, two ink pads and an original signed stamp picture.

From the late 1950s forward, the number of artists and writers using stamps in their works expanded tremendously and the range of works widened to include not only hand-stamped, limited edition books and prints but sculpture, paintings and multiples as well. In 1968, Multiples, Inc. (New York) published a project called *Stamped Indelibly,* containing work by such well-known artists as Marisol, Oldenburg, Warhol, Indiana and others.

Much of the stamp activity in the 1960s stemmed from the Fluxus movement, a loose-knit international avant group somewhat Dada in spirit, whose participants included Joseph Beuys, Robert Filliou, Ken Friedman, Dick Higgins, Yoko Ono and Ben Vautier. Vautier and Friedman are said to have published in 1966 the first multiple to include rubber stamps as physical objects. Published by Fluxus (New York), it was called *Fluxpost Kit* and contained stamps by both artists.

Even a partial listing of artists involved with stamp activities during the past several decades is a long one: Charles Amirkhanian, An-

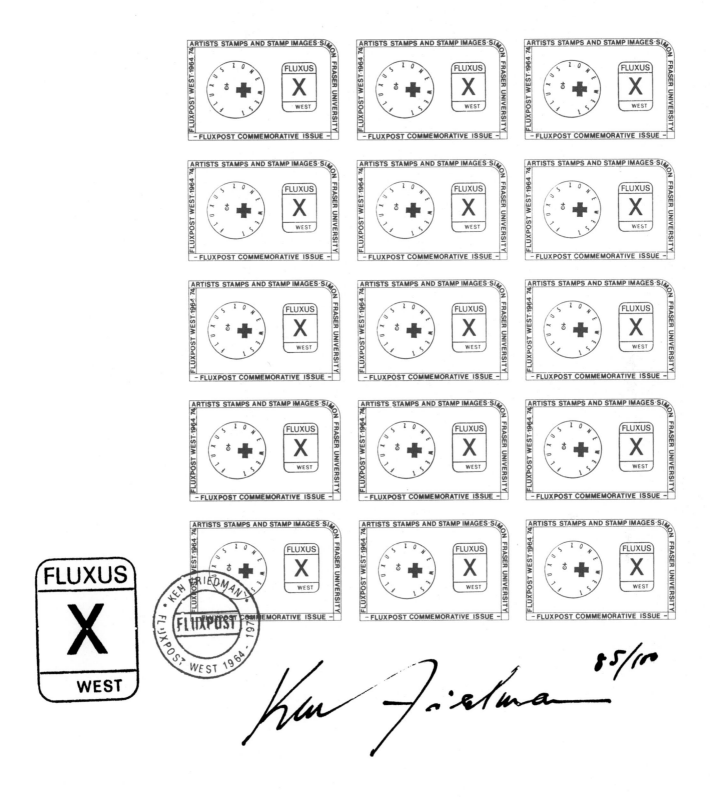

na Banana, George Brecht, Fletcher Coop, Hervé Fischer, Bill Gaglione, J.H. Kocman, Carol Law, G.J. de Rook, Daniel Spoerri, Pat Tavenner, Timm Ulrichs, Peter van Beveren, Emmett Williams and on and on. And then, of course, there is Saul Steinberg.

Wry Saul Steinberg, whose work appears frequently in *The New Yorker* magazine, has incorporated rubber stamps in his work for years, sometimes stamped in ink, sometimes in oil paint. A major Steinberg exhibit organized by the Whitney Museum of American Art contained numerous pieces dotted with the rubber stamps Steinberg considers to be highly personal. A book, *Saul Steinberg* by Harold Rosenberg (published by Alfred A. Knopf, Inc., New York), has been published in conjunction with the exhibit, and numerous pieces shown in it contain rubber stamps. Rosenberg's text notes that "Steinberg's studio today stocks enough rubber stamps to put him safely around the entire cosmos."

Since little has been written on rubber stamps and the artist, two books are especially important to know about. According to the Friedman/Gugelberger article in *Front,* Czech artist J. H. Kocman's book *Stamp Activity,* published in a limited, thirty-copy edition in 1972, was "the first true anthology of stamps and their use by

*"A Ready-Hand-Novel" was not only the first completely rubber-stamped literary work but also the first rubber-stamped novel.*

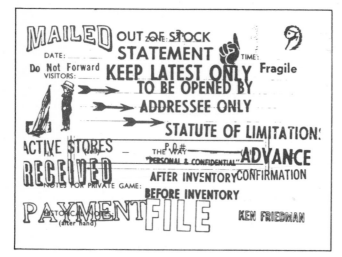

artists." It included the work of twenty-five artists. To say the book is as scarce as hen's teeth is no understatement, so chances of getting to see it are pretty remote.

A more accessible book, Hervé Fischer's *Art et Communication Marginale, Tampons D'Artistes,* was published by Editions, Andre Balland (Paris) in 1974. It is not exactly your superior printing job, but it *was* the pioneering effort to present an encyclopedic overview of stamp activity around the world and devotes almost two-hundred pages to whole stamp works or selections from artists' stamp collections. In most cases, brief biographical information about the artist is also supplied. Normal mortals may encounter some difficulty with the art jargon, and sometimes the translation is peculiar (the meaty stuff—the introduction—is fourteen pages long and in three languages); but overall it is interesting, especially a section in which Fischer attempts to create a typology (systematic classification) of stamp activity. He breaks it down as: Theme of Communication, Counter-Institutions, Protest, Various Statements of Values, Numbering, Certifications, Appropriations, Prints, Science, Visual Poetry, Works of Art and Playful Activity.

*The Rubber Stamp Album,* and our own zany feelings about stamps, must fall under Playful Activity, the least scary sounding of the lot. Only the most extensive and complete art libraries will have a copy of Fischer's book. Ecart Publications, rue Plantamour 6, CH-1201 Geneve, Switzerland, is said to be issuing a revised and expanded edition sometime in the near future, so you might want to drop a note to them requesting information on how to order it.

At least one other book devoted exclusively to rubber stamps and their relationship to art is said to be in the works on the West Coast.

So . . . innumerable artists are using rubber stamps as a primary medium while some are using them in conjunction with other materials. Some even turn the physical stamp itself into a work of art. As an artist's tool, rubber stamps have great appeal. They are relatively inexpensive, don't run or wear out and are easy to store or move. And, of course, a stamp impression in and of itself is really a print.

Neither the recognition of stamps in art nor the exhibit attention allotted to Rubber Stamp Art is in proportion to the volume of artistic stamp activity going on around the world. Hopefully, the pioneer efforts of Hervé Fischer (Paris), La Mamelle (San Francisco), Stempelplaats (Amsterdam), Other Books and So (Amsterdam), Ecart Publications (Switzerland), etc. will inspire new and wider recognition of rubber stamp activities.

We feel we've barely begun to scratch the surface, but feast your eyes on a sampling of what we've discovered.

Leavenworth Jackson "arrived in San Francisco, January 9, 1974, having graduated from the University of Michigan with all due process, fanfare and the realization that (contrary to rote) magic and illusion are no more results of sensoreal manipulation than the daily jazz which is generally served up as the truth."

Her drawings with stamps are surreal and capricious. They have been known to grace the pages of *New York*, *The New York Times*, *Psychology Today*, *Ms*, the *Village Voice*, *Saturday Review*, and the *YIPster Times*.

Bob Grimes of Patrick & Company was the recipient of one of Leavenworth's earliest stamp creations—a small book made with Patrick & Company stamps, each hand colored. Grimes used to carry it around in his pocket to show people what could be done with stamps.

In addition to freelance illustration and graphic design with rubber stamps (she is one of the few right now who actually makes a living playing with stamps), Leavenworth also sells a few of her creations. An odd poster called "Perserverance Furthers" is $7 postpaid; a booklet *Do Not Bend: a Rubber Stamped Romance* (for adults only) is $2 and includes one small original stamping. Then, of course, if you really want something unusual, there are custom-stamped erotic flip books for approximately $40 each, signed by the artist. To place orders write Leavenworth at 145 Waverly Place, N.Y.C. 10014.

*Portions of "Perserverance Furthers" by Leavenworth Jackson.*

*Map of Fire Island, N.Y. by Leavenworth Jackson*

**Shown opposite - pages from the book Leavenworth Jackson made for Bob Grimes of Patrick & Co.**

*Rona Dacoscos combined "found" stamps with some from a Japanese novelty set in a book made for Lynn Mechanic.*

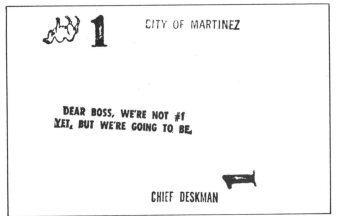

CITY OF MARTINEZ

**1**

DEAR BOSS, WE'RE NOT #1
YET, BUT WE'RE GOING TO BE.

CHIEF DESKMAN

88 X 888 . 3
88 X 888 . 4
88 X 888 . 5
88 X 888 . 6
88 X 888 . 7

88 X 888 . 8

WEST END

LOOP RES.
GRD. RES.
DATE    9·18·77

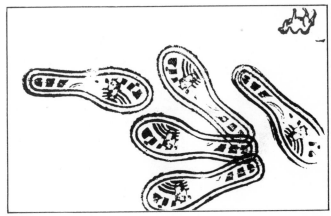

A. ☐  **SIEMENS TEST**

B. ☐ **SIEMENS TEST**

C. ☐ **SIEMENS TEST**

D. ☐ **SIEMENS TEST**

END

167

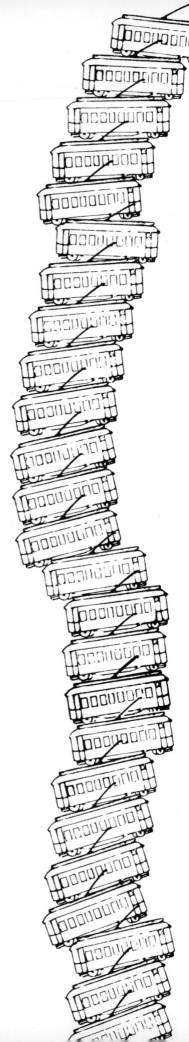

Poet Ray DiPalma is doing complex things with rubber stamps in a series of his own limited-edition handbound books and published paper objects. His works reflect efforts to get beyond the "You-stamp and-there-it-is" syndrome. A simple impression of an image is not what DiPalma is after in his work; he's constantly trying to find a way to make the stamps express his own ideas of space and form. He uses "the page as space," superimposing and sliding rubber-stamped images on each piece of the fine handmade papers of his books. Often the images have a narrative quality that is easily missed if you aren't looking for it . . . a stamped bus appears on one page and resurfaces, moved further on its journey, a few pages later.

The books are available from DiPalma himself at 226 West Twenty-first Street, Apartment 4-R, New York, New York 10011. Each book is hand-stamped in a very limited edition. Particularly interesting is a "Japanese Notebook:" an accordian (fold-out) notebook stamped in six colors of ink that opens to 4'8"x 6¼".

168

RAY DiPALMA

171

California artist Carol Law has worked and taught extensively in the area of photo plate-making for rubber stamps. The large halftone stamps used in her works are a result of experiment and research Law conducted with the cooperation of Walter Ellis of the H.R. Ellis Rubber Stamp Company, Berkeley, California.

Her works have been widely shown. She is included in Hervé Fischer's book *Art Et Communication Marginale* and she was a participant in the first international stamp-art exhibit in Paris in 1974.

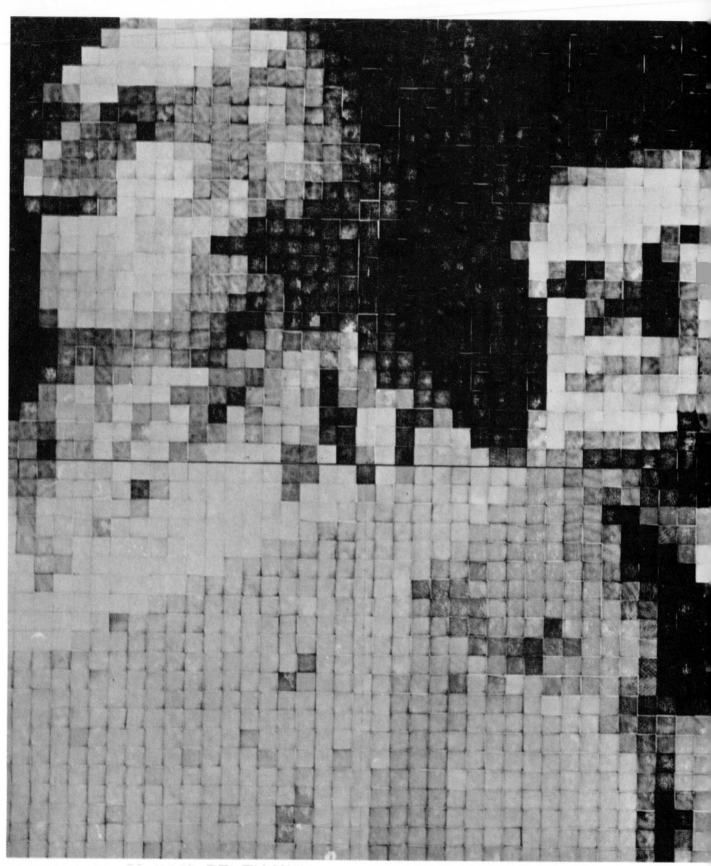

Obsessive Analog: For Gutson Borglum & Roosevelt Grier, *8' x 13', four panels, stamped by James Pomeroy in 1974.*

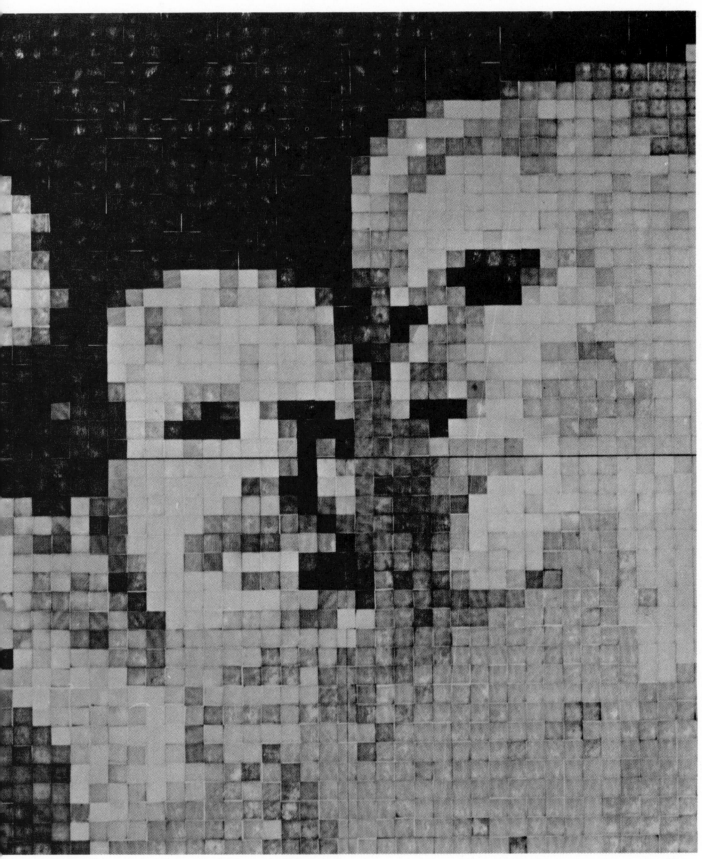

"*The piece is usually shown in a small room without much distance to back away. A reducing glass is placed on a table. Most people first view it as a large abstract composition and then realize it is Mt. Rushmore after viewing it through a lens.*"

175

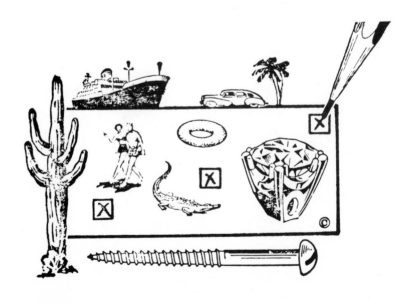

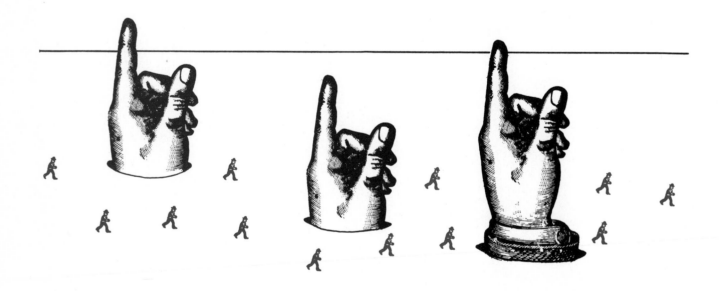

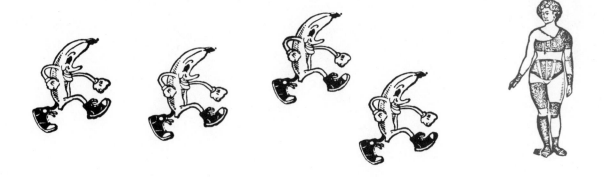

ANNA BANANA

STACY L. MANN

*Pamela Scesniak used the first stamp she had custom-made, called "Copulation of the Red Iguana," to create this piece.*

PIANTA DI VENEZIA: MILLEFIORI COMPUTRONIC *Bob Schimel (Director of Experimental Design Limited, Kent, Ohio) was inspired by computer graphics at M.I.T. and European glass paperweights. It took one month to execute*

182

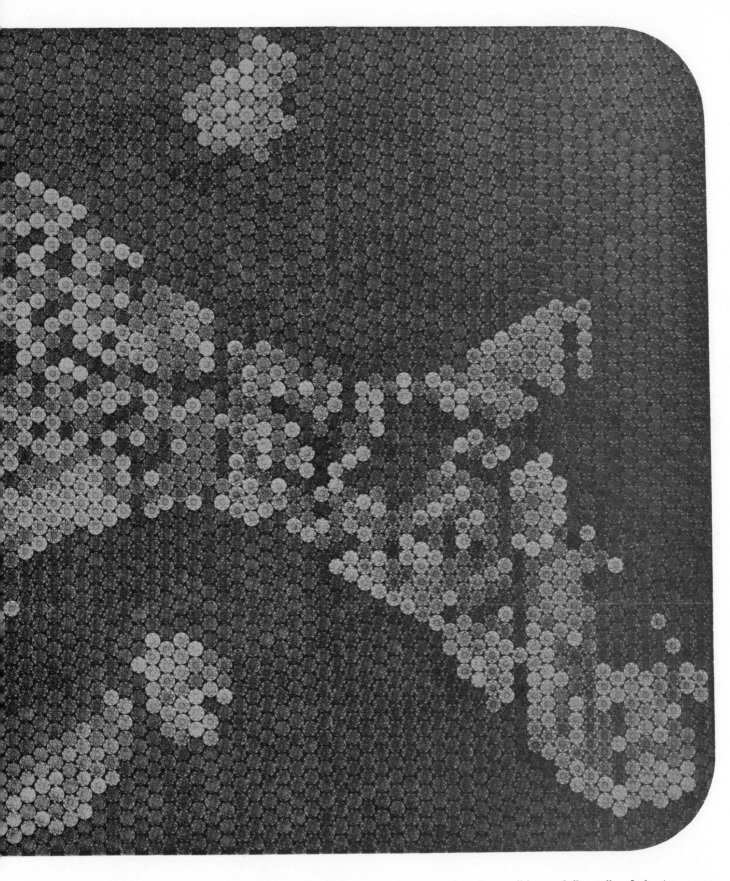

*this piece, which contains over 3,500 impressions and is 3' x 5'. The millefiori (means "thousand flowers" in Italian) rubber stamp used to create the piece is shown in actual size at the left.*

STAN ASKEW

**184**

STAN ASKEW

185

Going to Kansas city

Siamese Pot Roasts

2 Pot Roasts for every Girl! or Visa Versa!

The Pot Roast that ate Manhatten.

UFPR

[unidentified Flying pot Roaste]

"Le Pot Roaste de le Halston"

The Roast in fashion

Kiss me you big hunk of Pot Roast

oh yas honey!

Can a young woman from New Canaan find love in the kitchen?

186

DOUGLAS KELLEY

187

*"Crush"*

Paul M. Levy, a Boston artist of boundless energy, has a wide-ranging personal stamp collection and has been creating stamped artworks for years. The original design of his "Nut-and-bolt" appears on a piece of "big art" done in 1972 on a building in Cincinnati at Plum and West Fourth Streets. The nut and bolt motif appears frequently in his works. It's a halftone rubber stamp.

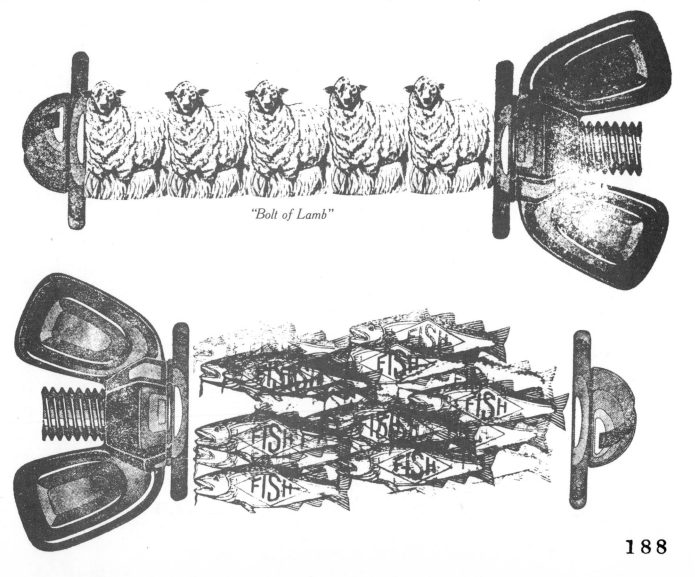

*"Bolt of Lamb"*

PAUL M. LEVY

189

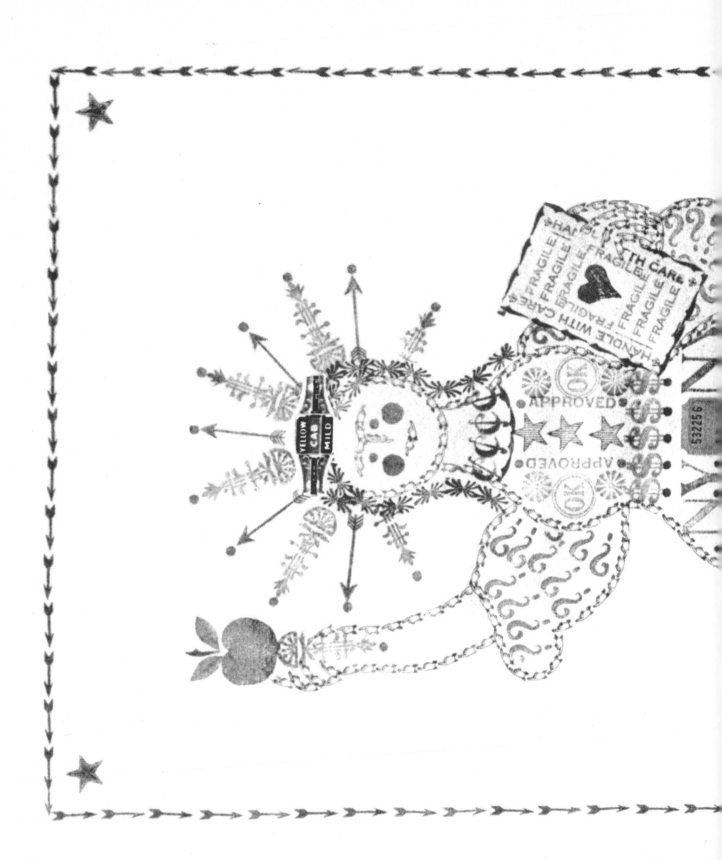

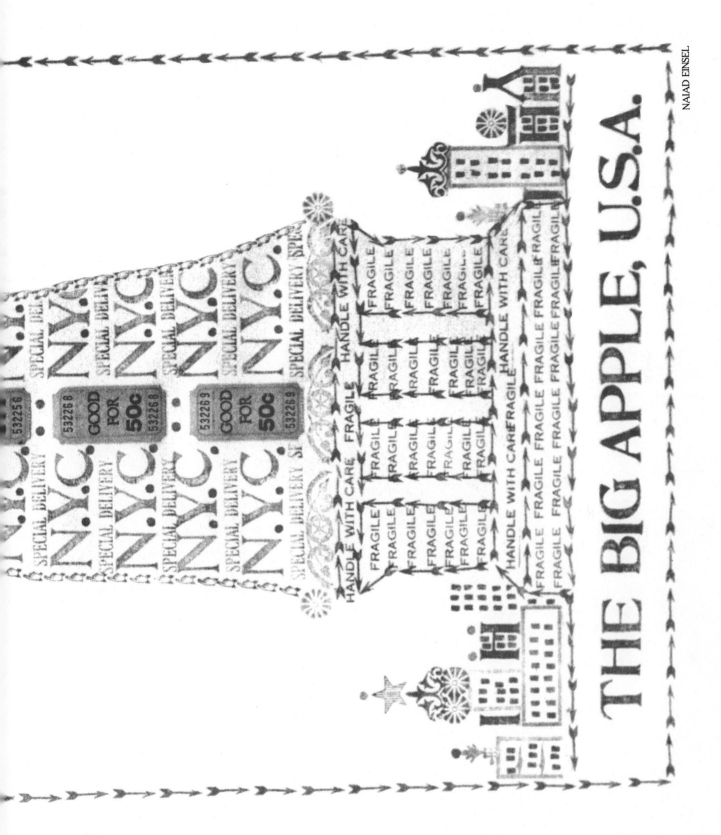

THE BIG APPLE, U.S.A.

191

## NOM DE PLUMES

№ 1    ARTIST
№ 2    ARTIST OF IDEAS
№ 3    ARTIST OF MANY MEDIA

№ 4    ARTIST OF UNKNOWN MEDIA
№ 5    MAIL QUEEN
№ 6    CHARM SCHOOL
№ 7    MUSEUM OF DELIGHTS
№ 8    PAT TAVENNER
№ 9    THE ALL AMERICAN GIRL

№ 10    THE PRACTICAL NURSE

№ 11    THE FARMERS DAUGHTER

№ 12    OAKLAND THE ETERNAL CITY

*Patricia Tavenner has used virtually every method of instant printing in her art since 1964. The "Nom De Plumes" rubber stamps were originally intended to grace envelopes; but as they grew as an autobiographical statement, she decided they were really meant to remain together on a single sheet. "Marie Bowes was compiling a book on women artists and didn't know how to categorize me, consequently I became the artist of unknown media category. I immediately had this made into a rubber stamp. The rest . . . had a natural evolution from this appropriate beginning." The "Nom De Plumes" are also used in Patricia's photographic postage stamps.*

NOM DE PLUMES № 9

NOM DE PLUMES № 10

NOM DE PLUMES № 7

193

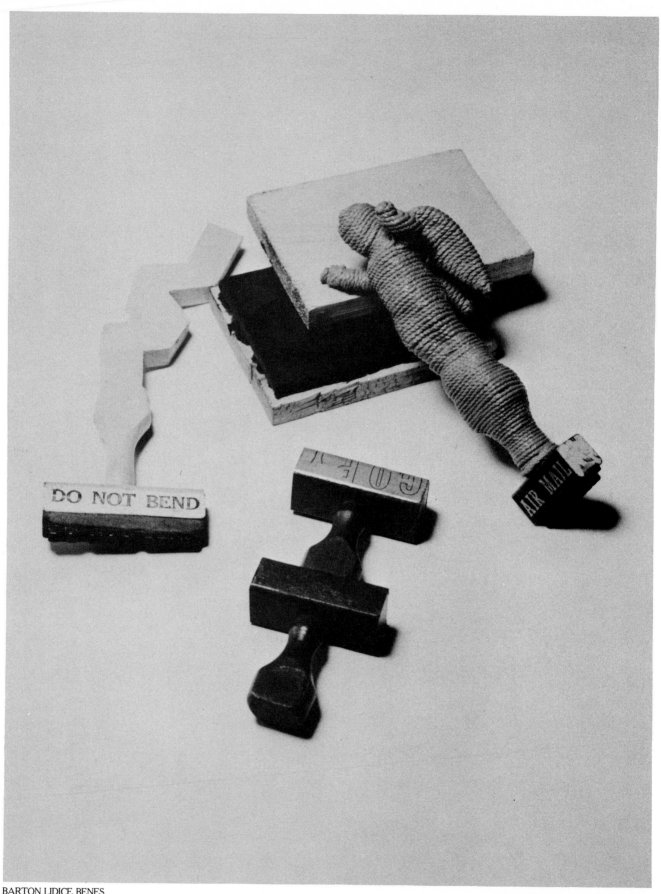

BARTON LIDICE BENES

*Michigan sculptor Jay Yager's works
reflect his interest in the relationship
between sculpture and printmaking. The
"Thumb" and "Hand" stamps are a
result. Yager says "Both have the
dimensional aspect of sculpture and the
potential to print." An impression made
with the "Hand" stamp was Yager's entry in the Third First International Rubber Stamp Art Exhibition.*

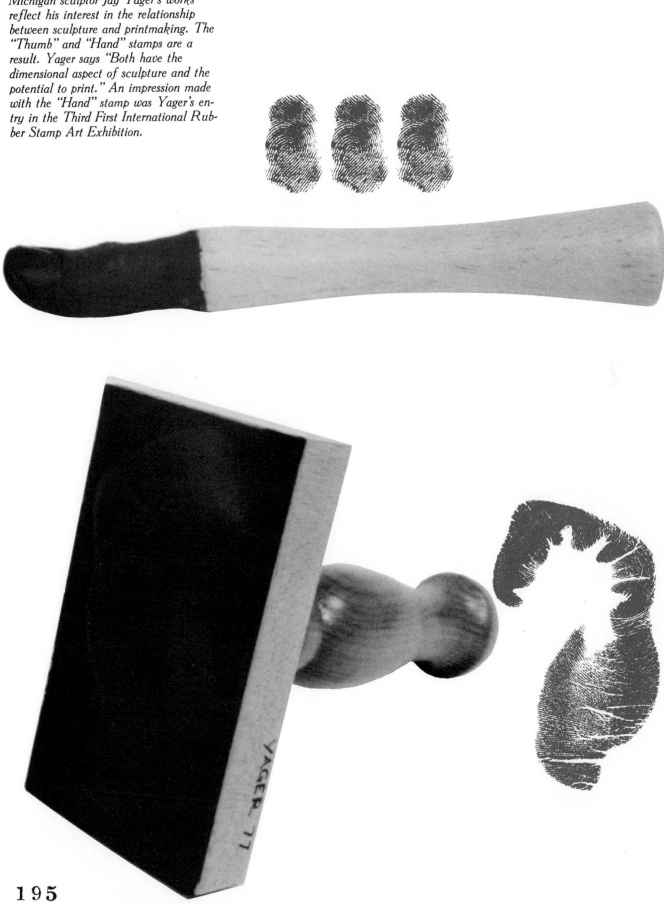

195

# CONTESTS & EXHIBITIONS

In 1917 the *Stamp Trade News,* trade periodical for the Marking Industry, made an attempt to rouse the latent artistic bent of stamp men by throwing a rubber-stamp contest. Rules were as follows, from the April 1917 issue:

> The stamp to be made shall be a plain handle rubber stamp (no cushion), to be used in printing on a card 3½" long and 2" wide, and to contain the following wording: John J. Maxwell Telephone Grand 724: Manufacturer of Rubber and Steel Stamps, Stencils, Checks, Seals, Box Printing, Plates, etc. 432 North Main Street, Columbus, Texas.

The magazine chose these somewhat mundane specifications for the stamp in hopes that the entries would prove even a simple text stamp could be made interesting with an inventive approach to display styles.

The three judges used a point system—forty points for composition, forty-five points for molding, fifteen points for mounting. Prizes were modest—first was three dollars and a year subscription to the *News,* second was two dollars and a subscription, and third was merely a subscription.

The entry deadline was April 15, 1917, and as is the case with most contests, entrants appear to have waited until the last minute to deluge the *News* with their handiwork. The three judges each chose a different stamp for first place. The two additional judges called into conference "didn't exactly clear the situation." The ensuing dialogue between judges dragged on for several months until the *News* finally decided the better part of valor was to give one dollar to each judge's first-prize choice in addition to the regular prizes. When it finally published the winning entries, the *News* was downright

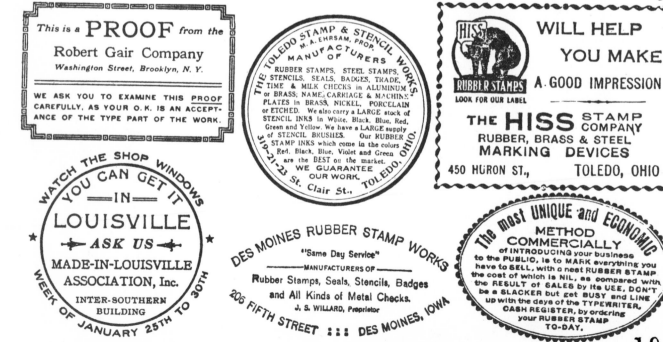

lyrical—"In the best stamps, the rubber was soft and velvety, of smooth surface and with the letters rising abruptly, clean, sharply outlined and regular." Descriptions of the polished wooden mounts and handles were effusive and dwelled in detail on the grain of the woods used.

Enthusiastic response to the contest was acknowledged swiftly as the *News* staged another, announced in November 1917. The ground rules were looser this time—wording was up to the entrant and the design could be square, rectangular, circular, oval, or any other that struck the entrant's fancy. More weight was put on "excellence of design, arrangement of type and appropriateness of typeface used." Winners of this competition showed a much livelier style than they did in the previous one.

Contest-happy, the *News* ran a third which closed on February 6, 1918. Winners were announced with the preface that "the illustrations will prove that rubber stamps can be handsomely designed and are worthy of use by the most fastidious upon almost any kind of paper work."

During the 1920s, the *News* ran a series of "library stamp" contests. These competitions brought in some dandy designs and the graphics continued to loosen, becoming increasingly more imaginative. The *News* reminded entrants that "this kind of rubber stamp is of small size and used as a book-mark for private libraries. Ovals or circles seem to be the favorite styles. . . ." The *News* also provided bits of psychological insight into the makeup of prospective purchasers of such stamps, noting "price as a rule is not a consideration as private libraries are owned by those of wealth and they consider a book-mark for some of their valuable works as quite important."

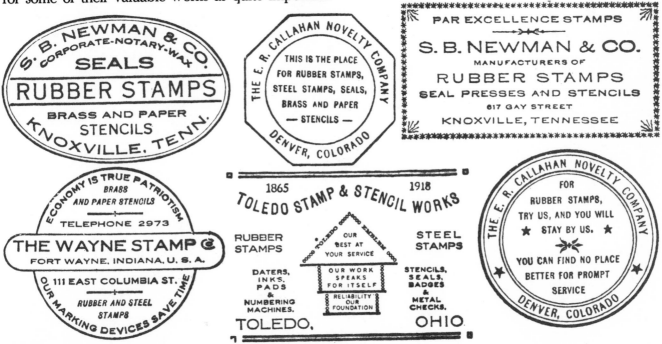

EX LIBRIS

There is no Frigate like a book to bear us lands away

EX LIBRIS
If thou art borrowed by a friend
Right welcome shall he be
To read, to study—not to lend—
But to return to me.

Property of PAUL REVERE LIBRARY Boston, Mass.

Private Library of Carroll B. Cary

CALGARY PUBLIC LIBRARY
BOOK No .............

LIBRARY OF JOHN I. SMITH KERRVILLE, TEXAS

LANGSIDE PUBLIC LIBRARY
Note
This book must be returned to the Library within ten days.

John Oliver Hay Library

PRIVATE LIBRARY OF HERMAN H. ROBBEN

READ AND BE WISE THE OWL LIBRARY

SELAH ELEMENTARY SCHOOL LIBRARY
Date............ No. .........

LIBRARY OF CHB 3849 Nic Ave

The Library of
Dr. Albert Clarence McKenzie

PRIVATE of W.H.L. S.F. LIBRARY

PRIVATE LIBRARY F. W. CRANZ BEAUMONT TEXAS

Library of Geo. I. Clark
Book No. _____

THE NEW SCHOLASTICISM CATHOLIC UNIVERSITY OF AMERICA WASHINGTON, D.C.

Library of William Haas Pittsburgh, Pa.

Private Library of John P. Benedict No.
Integros haurire fontes

Private Library NATHAN J. ORR BOOK NO. CASE SHELF

Property of Richmond Public Library Richmond, Va.

MUSIC LIBRARY OF MRS. WM. MARTINDALE Des Moines, Iowa No

LIBRARY OF A LINCOLN

LAW LIBRARY OF A. L SMITH BARRISTER Calgary - Alta.

Library of J. M. Brown

LIBRARY OF JOHN KING PHIL. PA.

A RENTS Free Library 220 S. Cherry RICHMOND

PROPERTY OF W. WORRALL BROOKLYN, N. Y.

LIBRARY OF W. H. LOHMANN

THE PROPERTY OF J. H. Dickinson CALGARY - ALTA.

LAW LIBRARY OF A. L SMITH BARRISTER Calgary - Alta.

Private Library NATHAN J ORR BOOK NO. CASE SHELF

Property of Henry J. Becker Hollis, L. I.

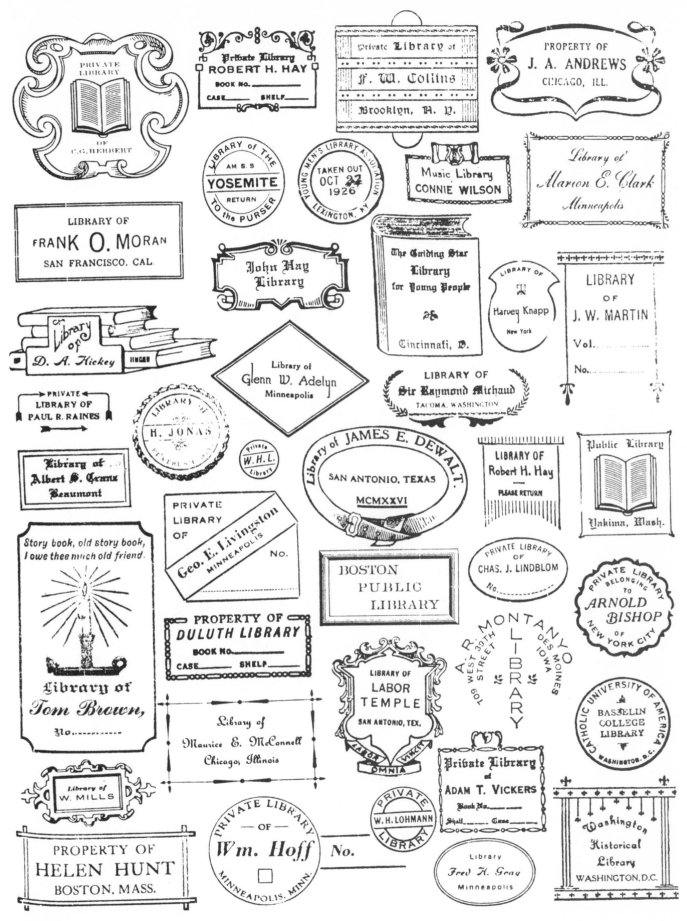

I AM GLAD IF I CAN STAMP — Endre Tót

The forum of Rubber Stamp Art exhibitions today is a far cry from what went on in the pages of *Stamp Trade News*. The first international exhibit of rubber-stamp works was originated by Hervé Fischer in May 1974, at the Institut de l'Environnement in Paris, France. Numerous others have followed, including one sponsored by Ecart in Geneva, Switzerland, one at the Simon Fraser Gallery in Burnaby, B.C., Canada, one organized by G.J. de Rook in 1975 in T'Hoogt, Holland and one sponsored by Other Books & So in 1976 in Amsterdam, Holland. The Big Island Gallery, Round Hill Road, Florida, New York, held a Rubber Stamp Art Convention in May of 1978 which contained a broad cross-section of art from established rubber-stamp artists as well as first attempts by a number of recent converts to the medium.

In October 1974, art professor Gael Bennett (known as Art Pig in certain circles) initiated the first in a series of exhibits that have since become annual events. Gael describes how it all began . . . "The First International Rubber Stamp Art Exhibition was conceived in a dingy Colorado honky-tonk late one evening by several art students and faculty at the University of Colorado, Colorado Springs, whose lot it was to be both drunk and angered at not having a regular exhibition space at the university. We wondered what kind of show could be had without a gallery. After considerable talk, we settled on the idea of an exhibit which could exist via the mails in various geographical locales unfettered by the narrow physical/temporal focus of the gallery/museum setting. At that time I had been involved with Correspondence Art for about a year and was quite enthusiastic about the alternative exhibition forms that flourish outside the establishment race track."

"The First International was *not* the First International, as I found out from numerous sources after putting the show together. As a result, we simply began appending the whole original title to the number of the year for which the show was scheduled. This seemed a logical way to save face through word manipulation."

Bennett was encouraged in the beginning "by such illustrious rubber-stamp heavyweights as Hervé Fischer and various correspondence/conceptual Dada artists, most notably Happy Edwin Golik Golikoff in Denver, Colorado, Ken Friedman of the Cosmic Flux, and obliquely by the late R. Mutt of Dada, California."

The Fourth First Annual International Rubber Stamp Art Exhibition took place in April 1978 at Old Dominion University, Norfolk, Virginia, where Bennett was guest teaching. Bennett was aided and abetted by Professor Ron Snapp, and the exhibit was twice the size of the first. Many of the entrants had been participating since 1974.

VOL. I NO. IV MAY 76/25¢ SF BAY AREA/50¢ ELSEWHERE

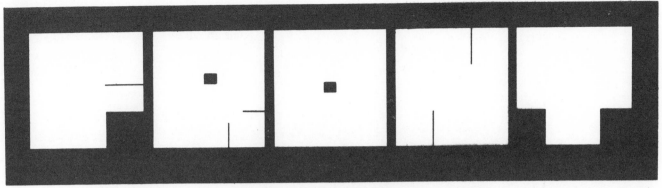

## Special Catalog Edition:
# INTERNATIONAL RUBBER STAMP — EXHIBITION

Bennett noted, "I am renewed and amazed each year I am involved with it. The spontaneous nature of the medium and general good will of the people who do rubber stamps is appealing to me. Stamp Art (among other forms) seems to provide a legitimate outlet for artists not wishing to dissipate their energies in the extra-art money/ego hussle. It has been my intention to maintain the show on this basis, ie., not letting it become too 'professional' or too exclusive. Everyone who enters is accepted and the economic focus is nonprofit. The selecting of prizewinners is intended simply as a means of funneling institutional money into individual artist's hands."

We hope you get a kick out of the samplings from the various years of the exhibition shown on pages 204-207.

**201**

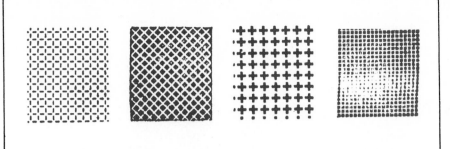

Continual Rubber Stamp Art exhibits are held in Amsterdam, Holland at Stempelplaats, St. Luciensteeg 25, which is a combination museum, art gallery, and workshop devoted to rubber-stamp activities. Their efforts are fully sponsored by Posthumus, Holland's oldest rubber-stamp manufacturer. It seems so right that a commercial rubber-stamp company should involve itself with stamps as an art form. We wish something like that would happen in America.

"Stempelplaats' curator, Aart van Barneveld, indicates that "the permanent collection of stamps and materials used to make them date from 1867."

Monthly exhibits feature the works of a single rubber-stamp artist. In the past several years, they have featured the work of Jonathan Held, Jr., Cozette de Charmoy, Robert Jacks, Peter van Beveren, Klaus Groh, Pawel Petasz, Barton Lidice Beneš, Ulises Carrion, Ray DiPalma, and Bill Gaglione. Stempelplaats' *Rubber* is "a monthly documenting the use of rubber stamps in the visual arts. Each issue, printed in an edition of 400, includes a short text on the work of the featured artist, a number of original stampings from works by the artist and several reproductions." A one-year subscription can be obtained by sending $12.50 via International Money Order *only.*

La Mamelle, Incorporated is heavily involved with rubber-stamp works in addition to their interest in video, audio, and "marginal" works. Partially funded by the National Endowment for the Arts, they generate a stream of fine publications, sponsor exhibits and workshops, and maintain, according to President Carl E. Loeffler, "the largest holding of rubber-stamp imprints on the West Coast," in their Contemporary Art Archives. In 1976, from April 23 through May 30, they held an International Rubber Stamp Exhibition with over 165 artists from around the world participating. A special catalog edition of their publication *Front* (Vol. 1, No. 4, May 1976) was devoted to covering the exhibit and contains some extremely interesting articles about rubber stamps and Stamp Art by Hervé Fischer, Ken Friedman, Georg M. Gugelberger, Klaus Groh, Carol Law, and E.M. Plunkett. Luckily, postpaid copies can still be obtained by sending La Mamelle $1.

**203**

BY TINKERBELL CERTIFIED

TINKERBELL

BEVERLY HODDINOTT

RICHARD KIRSTEN (DAIENSAI)

*Question Of The Month?*
*Where Will All Of The Mail Artists*
*Be When Mail Art Is No More?*

R. MUTT

ARE ONE INCH SQUARE

GARY UMSTATTD

VIRGINIA DAVIS

IRENE DOGMATIC

**They Laughed When I Sat Down
At the Piano
But When I Started to Play!~**

VICTOR NELSON

Yes, but will it fly?
LOWRY THOMPSON

JUNK IS ART—ART IS JUNK
PETER WHITSON WARREN

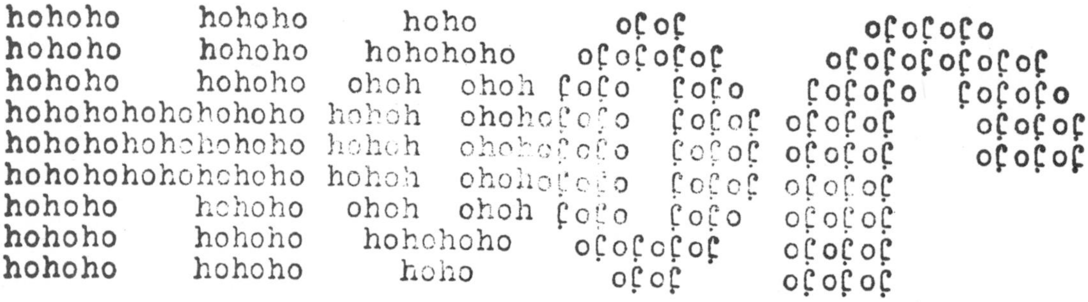

```
hohoho    hohoho      hoho        ofof          ofofofo
hohoho    hohoho      hohohoho     ofofofof      ofofofofofo
hohoho    hohoho      ohoh    ohoh fofo  fofo    fofofo   fofofo
hohohohohohohohoho    hohoh  ohohofofo fofof  ofofof     ofofof
hohohohohohohohoho    hohoh  ohohofofo fofof  ofofof     ofofof
hohohohohohohohoho    hohoh  ohohofofo fofof  ofofof
hohoho    hohoho      ohoh    ohoh fofo  fofo  ofofof
hohoho    hohoho      hohohoho     ofofofof     ofofof
hohoho    hohoho      hoho        ofof          ofofof
```

**I HAVE DRIVEN ACROSS THE U.S. FOUR TIMES AND HAVE NEVER EATEN IN A HOWARD JOHNSON'S.**

```
          jojojo      jojo-lois malone ohoho       ohohoh          ohohoh
          jojojo      jojojojo     ohohohoh         ohohoh          ohohoh
          jojojo   ojoj  ojoj   hoho hoho  ohohoh   ohohoh
          jojojo   jojoj  ojohohoho ohohoh ohohoh
jojojo    jojojo   jojoj  ojohohoho hohoh  ohohohohohohohoh
jojojo    jojojo   jojoj  ojohohoho hohoh  ohohohohohohohoh
ojojoj  ojojoj   ojoj  ojoj hoho  hoho  ohohoh   ohohoh
jojojojojojo     jojojojo   ohohohoho ohohoh     ohohoh
ojojojo          jojo         ohoh     ohohoh     ohohoh
```

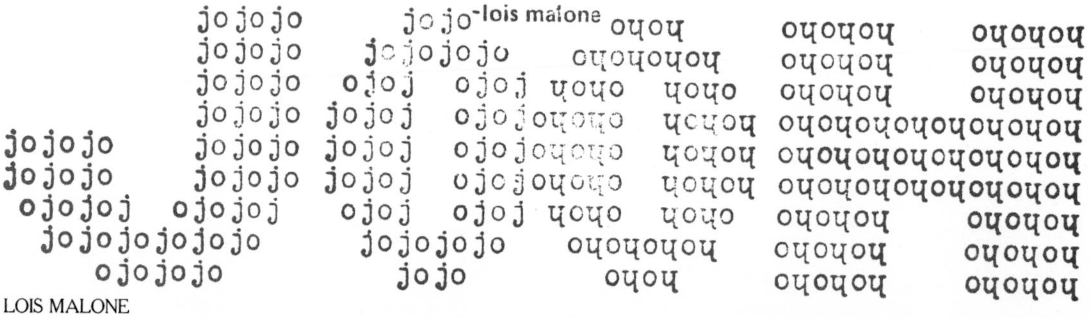

LOIS MALONE

204

M. BRICKELL

ELIZABETH A. SUTTON

I AM A RED PENCIL

## eg,

EILEEN GLASER

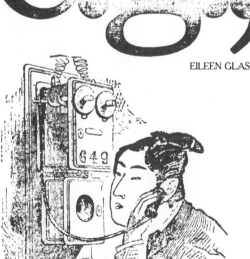

STEVEN TAKATA

Dear _____

I'm so sorry I ran out on you last night. I realized then what a fool I've been. It's hard to make these kind of social decisions. I thought about it all the way home... Well, believe me, I'm through with my tricks. You can count on it. I don't want to promise anything, but it's a new leaf. Next time I'll be able to make up my mind once and for all.

Sincerely,

_____

MONIQUE SAFFORD

THE SMELL OF MOTHBALLS IS
REPULSIVE TO SQUIRRELS

ROBERT L. ARNOLD

FOOT STAMP

ELIZABETH A. SUTTON

loose

lips

GAEL BENNETT

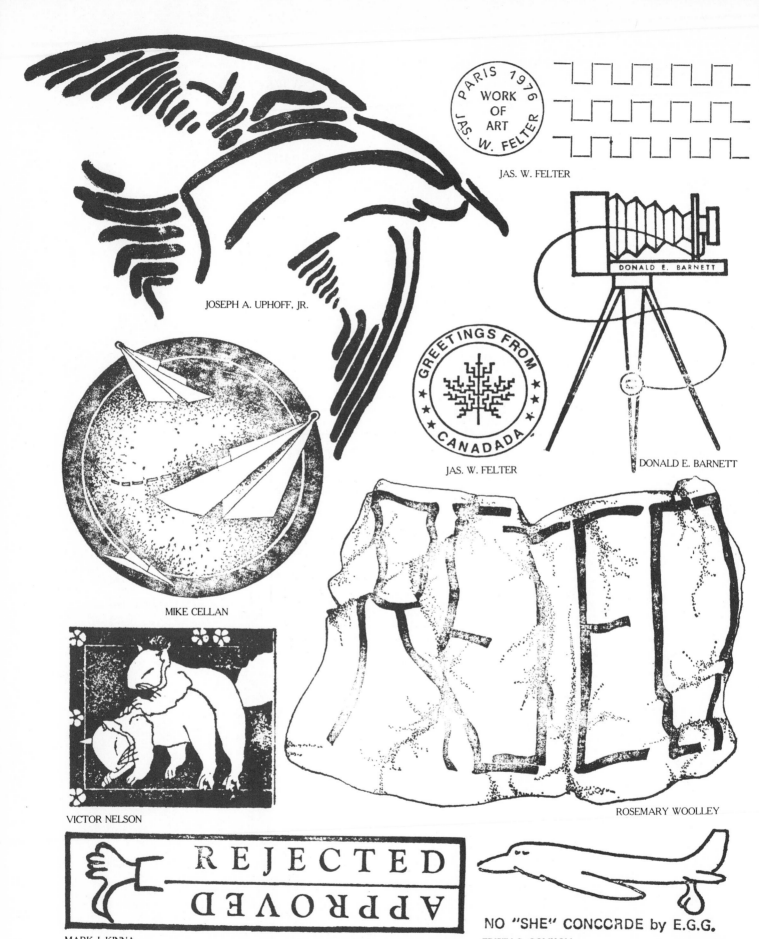

JAS. W. FELTER

JOSEPH A. UPHOFF, JR.

DONALD E. BARNETT

JAS. W. FELTER

MIKE CELLAN

ROSEMARY WOOLLEY

VICTOR NELSON

REJECTED

APPROVED

MARK J. KINNA

NO "SHE" CONCORDE by E.G.G.

EDWIN G. GOLIKOV

206

# NOT WORTH MUCH

MICHAEL MOLLETT

And let no one imagine because he has made merry in the warm tilth and quaint nooks of romance, that he can even guess at the austere and thrilling raptures of those who have climbed the cold, white peaks of art.

**Clive Bell**

ROBERT L. ARNOLD

KEN DALEY

Artist's Proof

K. MARY SMITH

R.E. GASOWSKI

MARY ANN MERKER-BENTON

AARON LEVENTHAL

## Identification

Robert Saunders
Box 631  Route 2
Weare, N.H. 03281

| O | Pos | 12/13/40 |
|---|-----|----------|
| M | 185 | 6-2 |

378 42 5085

Robert W. Saunders

37842

ROBERT SAUNDERS

NOTICE YOUR ATTENTION TO THIS

RON SNAPP

THE DEATH OF ROMANCE
By Jerry Dreva
February 14, 1977
So. Milwaukee, Wisconsin

JERRY DREVA

SPECIAL OK DELIVERY
PAULA K. YOUNKIN

NIKOLAI GREGORIC III

OFFICIAL SEAL CHICAGO SEAL

FIVE/CINQ AESTHETICS

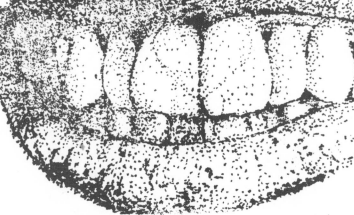

M. BRICKELL

*I really respect you as a person*

LIN FIFE

# RIP·OFF·ART

After a while, ordering stamps from rubber-stamp companies or tracking down stamp oddities in retail stores won't be sufficient for your stamping needs. This is the time to head to your local rubber-stamp company armed with some art work of your own and have a stamp custom made.

If you have the skills to do pen-and-ink drawings, you are home free, but most people can't draw their way out of a paper bag. The solution lies in the easy art of clipping. Nothing more than the ability to make a decision and use a pair of scissors is required to achieve one-of-a-kind personal stamps.

As you may recall from the chapter on how stamps are made, a rubber stamp can be made from any piece of clear, high-contrast black-and-white artwork. Where to find the art? Magazines abound with suitable drawings. Any copy of *The New Yorker, New York Magazine,* etc. is literally swarming with such art. Small cartoons, designs from packaging, brochures, and catalogs are all pregnant with free art.

For the most ideas in one place, we recommend a series of books published in inexpensive paper editions by Dover Publications called the Pictorial Archive Series. These books can be purchased from your local bookseller, ordered directly from Dover through their mail-order department or, if you live in New York City, purchased on the spot at their own showplace retail store at 180 Varick Street, New York, New York, on the ninth floor. If your local bookstore doesn't have the desired title in stock, they'll gladly special-order for you; or you can write directly to Dover at the Varick Street address and request a copy of their Dover Art Materials Catalog, which lists several hundred useful titles, many from the Pictorial Archive Series.

This important quote from the Dover catalog appears in the front of many of their titles: "Individual illustrations in these books are copyright-free, and may be used (usually up to ten items per occasion) without further payment, permission, or acknowledgement. You purchase rights when you buy the book." Other Dover titles, books from other publishers, and clippings from magazines are not copyright-free; so care must be taken about how the stamps that result from clippings are used.

The rule of thumb on clipping is that anything goes, regardless of the source, as long as you restrict the rubber stamp with the design to your own exclusive, personal use. You cannot sell the stamp or engage in commerce with it in any way. Sounds vaguely obscene, doesn't it? Keep your shirttails clean in this regard, and you can clip to your heart's content.

Some Dover titles that contain quantities of appealing clean

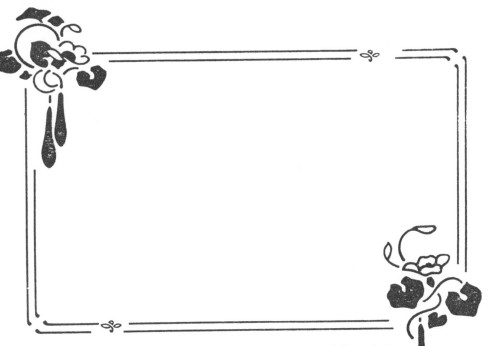

black-and-white art are; *Handbook of Pictorial Symbols* by Rudolf Modley ($3.50), a comprehensive source book of pictography. It shows over 3,250 internationally-used symbols for commonplace activities, and also roadsigns, etc. There are symbols for food, money, automobiles, restrooms, railway crossings, etc. These graphics are bold, with lots of solid background, so you'd want to make sure any stamp made from them is of rubber, not photo-polymer.

*Decorative Frames and Borders*, edited by Edmund V. Gillon, Jr. ($4), provides hundreds of lovely ways to frame a phrase or make borders for stationery in Art Deco, Art Nouveau, or Renaissance styles. There are 396 illustrations to choose from.

*Montgomery Ward & Co. Catalogue and Buyer's Guide*, No. 57, Spring and Summer 1895, is an unabridged replica of the real thing. "One picture is worth a thousand words" was the operating philosophy of the catalog. It is chock-full of tiny black-and-white illustrations of everything from inlaid wooden boxes and bone dice to swatches of human hair and spooky doll heads. You could go bankrupt trying to have a stamp made of everything intriguing in this $8.50 treasure.

*Cartouches and Decorative Small Frames*, edited by Edmund V. Gillon, Jr. ($3), has some really fetching (Gothic, Art Deco—and beyond—) designs. One in particular, a cupid with a letter suspended from his neck, would be colossal to stamp on valentines.

*Victorian Frames, Borders and Cuts* ($3) is the best Dover bargain. It has more border designs than there are places to use them, as well as 268 pictorial cuts of various trades, from brewer to gent's furnishings, plus gobs of scrollwork.

Dover isn't the only publisher doing books that are reasonably priced and have good stamp-oriented art. Bellerophon Books publishes a slew of wonderful coloring books. Most book stores have a revolving rack with a good assortment. The artwork in these is too big to just clip out and use, but it is very easy to ask any stamp company to enlarge or reduce a design. These would definitely have to be reduced unless you wanted to end up with stamps the size of the monster that devoured Cleveland. Write Bellerophon for a free brochure of their offerings! 153 Stewart St., San Francisco, California 94105.

Another publisher, Hastings House, specializes in books for graphic arts and advertising types. Most of the titles are published in expensive hardcover editions (from $15 to $30), so clipping from their books may be a temptation you can resist. Look at them in a library or book store before investing.

Publisher Harold Hart created his series of reasonably priced paperback clip-books several years ago. It's called the Hart Design Archive, and each book contains public-domain designs which can be used without fee or permission. Prices are higher than those for Dover books and many of the designs are halftones, so choose with care. *Borders and Frames* ($8.95) has fabulous border designs of acorns, tiny hearts, castles, maple leaves, and the like. *Humor, Wit & Fantasy* ($14.95) provides over 2,000 public domain pictures. The section devoted to fantasy initials is inspiring. *The Animal Kingdom*

(14.95) is a potpourri of over 2,200 animal illustrations. The idea of an eccentric personal logo of an aardwolf or hook-billed creeper has merit.

Having stamps custom made is, of course, more expensive than ordering existing stamps. Any commercial stamp company listed in the Yellow Pages will make one up for you. Prices are contingent on the size of the stamp, whether or not an actual cut or black-and-white artwork is supplied, and how fast the stamp is wanted. Average price is between $8 and $15. Many of the companies listed in the catalog section welcome special orders. Send a photocopy of what you'd like and request an estimate.

The cheapest type of custom stamp is one with a word or phrase. Stamp companies have various typefaces available, and price is based on the size type chosen and final size of the stamp. Average cost is between $3.50 and $5. Phrase stamps fill the void in a unique way for special occasion gifts. Instead of a card, send a rubber stamp that says HAPPY BIRTHDAY.

Interesting stamps can be made from any printer's cut in good condition. A cut is an engraved block or sheet used for printing. It is generally made of metal, although very old ones were hand carved out of wood. Cuts occasionally turn up at swap-meets and flea markets or can be purchased at stores specializing in selling old printing paraphernalia. Watch for printing plants being dissolved. Or find a printer or type house converting from "hot" (metal) to "cold" (film) type. They may sell you some metal cuts.

Supplying a cut to the stamp maker eliminates one step in the manufacturing process and should result in a saving to you. Exactly how much depends on the company, so question them shrewdly. If the stamp is being made of photo-polymer, you won't save anything since the process doesn't require a mold be made first. If you supply only artwork for a rubber stamp, a cut is made and returned to you along with the actual rubber stamp. Don't throw cuts out when you get them back. Trade with other stamp collectors . . . or use them if you decide to order more of the same.

**211**

# PSSSSST!... SECRET SOURCES REVEALED

## STORES CARRYING STAMPS

**KAILL FINE CRAFTS**
Juneau, Alaska 99803

**THE CARD FACTORY**
7650 Sunset Boulevard
Los Angeles, California 90046

**THE CARD FACTORY**
8910 Santa Monica Boulevard
Los Angeles, California 90069

**CARGO WEST**
5280 East Second Street
Long Beach, California 90803

**CENTERING**
231 "G" Street
Davis, California 95616

**CHICKEN LITTLE EMPORIUM**
1108 Polk Street
San Francisco, California 94109

**CRAFT AND FOLK ART MUSEUM**
5814 Wilshire Boulevard
Los Angeles, California 90036

**THE CRAFT GALLERY**
126 San Jose Avenue
Capitola, California 95010

**DEJA-VU**
1979 Shattuck
Berkeley, California 94704

**THE GREAT ACORN**
800 San Anselmo Avenue
San Anselmo, California 94960

**GREETINGS**
4125 Piedmont Avenue
Oakland, California 94611

**HABITAT**
3895 18th Street
San Francisco, California 94114

**THE HANDCRAFTER**
6 Petaluma Boulevard
Petaluma, California 94952

**INCESTUOUS RUBBER STAMP
COMPANY**
Main Street Arcade
Mendocino, California 95460

**L'ARK**
647 San Anselmo Avenue
San Anselmo, California 94960

**MR. MOPPS**
1405 Grove Street
Berkeley, California 94709

**MARY STRICKLER'S QUILT**
936 "B" Street
San Rafael, California 94901

**THE NATURE COMPANY**
1999 El Dorado
Berkeley, California 94707

**THE NATURE COMPANY**
2836 College Avenue
Berkeley, California 94705

**NINEPATCH**
2001 Hopkins
Berkeley, California 94707

**PAPERBACK TRAFFIC**
535 Castro
San Francisco, California 94114

**PATIENCE CORNERS**
1382 Solano Avenue
Albany, California 94706

**PENTIMENTO**
4273 California
San Francisco, California 94118

**POCKETFUL OF RAINBOWS**
115 Fourth Street
Santa Rosa, California 95401

**PROPINQUITY**
8915 Santa Monica Boulevard
West Hollywood, California 90069

**RAINBOW'S END**
Cooper House
Santa Cruz, California 95060

**SAN FRANCISCO MUSEUM
OF MODERN ART**
Van Ness at McAllister
San Francisco, California 94102

**THE SOAP PLANT**
3720 Sunset Boulevard
Los Angeles, California 90026

**THE SHOPPING BAG**
15 Caperton Avenue
Piedmont, California 94611

**UNIVERSITY OF CALIFORNIA ART
MUSEUM BOOKSTORE**
2625 Durant Avenue
Berkeley, California 94720

**THE WOODEN HORSE**
110 Cooper Street
Santa Cruz, California 95060

**THE BODY SCENTER**
1618 Wisconsin Avenue NW
Washington, D.C. 20007

**THE WRITTEN WORD**
1054 31st Street NW
Washington, D.C. 20016

**SPARKLE PLENTY**
5819 Sunset Drive
South Miami, Florida 33143

**CHARRETTE (Clearstamps™ only)**
31 Olympia Avenue
Woburn, Massachusetts 01801

1 Winthrop Square
Boston, Massachusetts 02110

44 Brattle Street
Cambridge, Massachusetts 02138

**GOODS DEPT. STORE**
11 Boylston Street
Cambridge, Massachusetts 02138

**THE PAPERBACK TRADER**
653 Grand Avenue
St. Paul, Minnesota 55105

**ALBRIGHT-KNOX GALLERY SHOP**
Buffalo, New York 14222

**ANY OCCASION**
209 Columbus Avenue
New York, New York 10023

**CHARRETTE (Clearstamps™ only)**
212 East 54th Street
New York, New York 10022

**GREETINGS**
35 Christopher Street
New York, New York 10014

**JENNY B. GOODE**
1194 Lexington Avenue
New York, New York 10028

**JOHNNY JUPITER**
392 Bleecker Street
New York, New York 10014

**MYTHOLOGY**
370 Columbus Avenue
New York, New York 10024

**PIZAZZ**
811 Lexington Avenue
New York, New York 10021

**PROPS AND PRACTICALS**
150 West 52nd Street
New York, New York 10019

**RUELLE'S**
321 Columbus Avenue
New York, New York 10023

**HAND OF THE CRAFTSMAN**
58 South Broadway
Nyack, New York 10960

**UNCLE ELI'S**
129 North Beaver
State College,
Pennsylvania 16801

**NATURAL WOMAN**
281-B Thayer Street
Providence,
Rhode Island 02906

**FOLK TOY**
809 Rio Grande
Austin, Texas 78701

**UNICORN GALLERY**
25 Dobie Mall
Austin, Texas 78705

**SALMAGUNDI FARMS**
185 South State Highway 525
Coupeville, Washington 98239

**IN THE BEGINNING**
301 East Pine Street
Seattle, Washington 98122

**THE PEACH TREE CRAFT SHOP
AND GALLERY**
4518 University Way NE
Seattle, Washington 98105

**JOHN MICHAEL KOHLER
ARTS CENTER**
608 New York Avenue
Sheboygan, Wisconsin 53081

**GREAT EXPECTATIONS**
65 South Glenwood
Jackson, Wyoming 83001

# STAMPS & SUNDRIES

**KEN ART**
RD 1
Whitehouse Station, New Jersey 08889
Free catalog of stock rubber stamps and logos.

**BEEHIVE ENTERPRISES**
P.O. Box 87
Williamsbridge Station
Bronx, New York 10467
$0.25 brochure features a wide variety of feminist gifts including two feminist symbol rubber stamps. Each stamp is $2.75, postpaid.

**BARTON LIDICE BENEŠ**
463 West Street
956 H
New York, New York 10014
A set of ten pleasantly oddball rubber-stamped postcards called "Holy Cards" are available directly from the artist for $11 per set, postpaid. Each card is rubber-stamped, and a meaningful portion of the design has been cut away (holes, get it?): the car has its windows cut out, etc. Sets are in a stamped envelope signed by the artist.

**COLIN BRAND**
Modern Printing
51 Hampton Road
Keswick, South Australia 5035
An Australian manufacturer of interesting rubber stamps. Write for details.

**BROOKSTONE COMPANY CATALOG**
127 Vose Farm Road
Peterborough, New Hampshire 03458
A free sixty-eight page catalog of hard-to-find tools and other fine things includes a listing for reasonably-priced assortments of cherry and walnut wood blocks which would make very handsome rubber-stamp mountings. Each assortment contains fourteen pieces of wood and costs around $9. Send for catalog before ordering.

**DONNELLY/COLT**
Box 271
New Vernon, New Jersey 07976
Free brochure of "Anti-Nuke" bumper stickers, buttons and . . . two rubber stamps. Each stamp is $2.25, postpaid.

**HERCULES INCORPORATED**
Graphic Systems Business Center
910 Market Street
Wilmington, Delaware 19899
Manufacturer of Merigraph® Photorelief Printing Plate System for making polymer stamps.

**JOANNE HOFFMAN**
227 Fitzwater Street
Philadelphia, Pennsylvania 19147
Joanne is a freelance graphic designer who'll rubber-stamp anything from t-shirts to belts to order. Drop her a note for information on prices and designs. (see pg. 81)

**HORCHOW COLLECTION™**
P.O. Box 34257
Dallas, Texas 75234
A slick, elegant mail-order catalog that once offered a memorable jungle animal rubber-stamp set. You never know, they might offer it again sometime.

**INDIA INK GALLERY**
1231 Fourth Street
Santa Monica, California 90401
The gallery has a handsome 18″ by 24″ poster of a rubber-stamped oriental rug by Barton Lidice Benes. The poster announces a Benes exhibit and is $9, postpaid.

**JAAP RIETMAN ART, Inc.**
167 Spring Street
New York, New York 10012
A specialty bookstore devoted to art books. They've been known to have difficult to find European books and art periodicals that have information on rubber stamps.

**KTAV PUBLISHING COMPANY**
75 Varrick Street
New York, New York 10013
KTAV stocks a Hebrew Alphabet Set of rubber stamps (unmounted) that are designed primarily for use by children. The set (62 symbols and characters) is $3, postpaid.

**KING BRAND MUSIC PAPERS, INC.**
1595 Broadway
New York, New York 10019
This music supply house stocks rubber stamps designed for use on musical scores. The stamps say things like "flugelhorn," "alto" and "bassoon." Send a stamped, self-addressed envelope when requesting a copy of their free catalog sheets and price list.

**FLOYD MALAN STAMPS**
P.O. Box 2319
Lancaster, California 93534
An inexpensive source for custom-made rubber stamps through the mail. Send stamped, self-addressed envelope for free brochure.

**TOMMY MEW**
Director, Fluxus West/
Southeast
Department of Art
Berry College
Mt. Berry, Georgia 30149

In an ongoing effort to keep the spirit of the Fluxus goings-on expanding, two of the best-known stamps in the world are for sale from time to time. They are the "Fluxus West" and "Fluxus/Southeast" stamps. Cost is approximately $7.50 per stamp. Inquire about availability and exact cost before attempting to order.

**nomoma**
P.O. Box 1048
Amherst, Massachusetts 01002
This is a basement rubber-stamp operation being run by three delightful mail-art crazies who have used rubber stamps in their art for years. Write them for ordering information.

**LOWRY THOMPSON**
29 East Avenue
New Canaan,
Connecticut 06840
Lowry is making splendid
rubber-stamped
stationery and postcards.
Write for ordering
details.

**NAOMI SAFELY**
Route 2, Box 40C
Rockwell City, Iowa 50579
Naomi runs her rubber-stamp catalog from a wheelchair and makes all of the stamps in her own home. The designs are similar to those manufactured by Decor-8-Craft and are meant to be used primarily to decorate stationery and greeting cards. Her one-hundred-page catalog is $1.65. Supplements to the catalog are published regularly.

**STONEHAND**
245 Centre Street
New York, New York 10013
"New York's graphic boutique" stocks a vast assortment of printer's cuts, wood type, wood cuts, etc. This is a retail store, so no catalog is available. If you are looking for something specific, however, you might consider dropping them a note of inquiry.

**TRIFLES**
P.O. Box 44432
Dallas, Texas 75234
The free Trifles mail-order catalog is a potpourri of interesting gifts. Now and then a rubber-stamp set is included.

**UNTITLED**
159 Prince Street
New York, New York 10012
Specialize in modern art postcards and greeting cards. Sometimes they stock rubber-stamped art postcards.

**WHITE MARE**
Preston Hollow, New York 12469
White Mare, a feminist concern, currently has one rubber stamp available and more are planned. The CHAI stamp, designed by Liza Cowan, is a combination of symbols signifying Jewish feminism. The stamp is $4, postpaid.

**WALTER WINGERTER**
P.O. Box 676
Elmhurst, New York 11373
An inexpensive mail-order source for custom-made rubber stamps. The free brochure will not fit inside a standard-size envelope, so be sure to include a postage stamp with your request rather than a stamped, self-addressed envelope.

**LILLIAN VERNON™**
510 South Fulton Avenue
Mt. Vernon, New York 10550
Free mail-order catalog of gifts. This is a source for blank jigsaw-puzzle letters.
(see pg. 76)

# ARCHIVES BOOKSTORES MUSEUMS

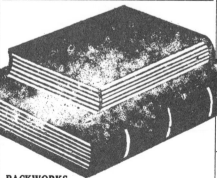

**BACKWORKS**
488 Greenwich Street
New York, New York 10013
A bookstore, devoted to the documentation of Fluxus works and mail art.

**FRANKLIN FURNACE**
112 Franklin Street
New York, New York
An archive of contemporary art publications open to the public. Many of the publications contain rubber-stamp works.

**JEAN BROWN ARCHIVE**
Shaker Seed House
Tyringham, Massachusetts 01264
An amazing archive of Surrealist, Dada and Fluxus material. Archive is not open to the general public although it is open to serious students if arrangements are made in advance.

**OTHER BOOKS AND SO**
Herengracht 227
Amsterdam, Holland
A gallery/shop devoted to books by artists.

**PRINTED MATTER**
7 Lispenard Street
New York, New York 10013
A bookstore specializing in artists' books including rubber-stamped books by Ray DiPalma, Robert Jacks, etc.

**THE RUBBER STAMP MUSEUM**
Institute for Advanced Studies
in Contemporary Art
6361 Elmhurst Drive
San Diego, California 92120
The Rubber Stamp Museum, which has a collection of over 1,400 rubber stamps, is not open to the general public. Serious students may gain access by arranging an appointment through the Institute's Dr. Kenneth S. Friedman.

**STEMPELPLAATS**
St. Luciensteeg 25
Amsterdam, Holland
A museum/gallery/bookstore sponsored by Hollands oldest rubber-stamp company.

# BOOKS AND PERIODICALS

**FIRST DAYS: JOURNAL OF THE AMERICAN FIRST DAY COVER SOCIETY**
c/o S. Koved, Editor
14 Samoset Road
Cranford, New Jersey 07016
A bi-monthly periodical devoted to the ad-

vancement of First Day Cover collecting. Send stamped, self-addressed envelope for subscription information. It sometimes contains information on rubber-stamp cachets.

## A GIRL NAMED HERO
written and illustrated by Kit Duane.
Rubber Stamp Art by Jackie Leventhal.
A feminist children's story containing rubber-stamped illustrations. Available $3 postpaid from Kelsey Press, 2824 Kelsey Street, Berkeley, California 94705. The rubber stamps used to illustrate the book are still available and ordering instructions for the stamps are on the back cover of the book.

## IMAGEZINE
La Mamelle, Inc.
P.O. Box 3123
San Francisco, California 94119
This "magazine" is actually a rubber stamp. Each issue is $15. Inquire about availability before attempting to order.

## MARKING PRODUCTS AND EQUIPMENT
c/o Marking Industry Magazine
666 Lakeshore Drive
Chicago, Illinois 60611
A complete name and address guide to marking device manufacturers and companies. Revised annually. $3 per copy, postpaid.

## RUBBER
Stempelplaats
St. Luciensteeg 25
Amsterdam, Holland
A monthly leaflet-style periodical documenting the use of rubber stamps in the visual arts. Subscription rate is $12.50 per year (payment by International Money Order *only*).

## STAMP ART
edited by G.J. de Rook.
Other Books and So
Herengracht 259
Amsterdam, Holland
A catalog published on the occasion of the STAMP ART SHOW held at Other Books and So from April 27 through May 15, 1976. Write for ordering information.

## STEMPELKUNST
by G.J. De Rook.
Ex/press
P.O. Box 14012
Utrecht, Holland
Book containing rubber-stamp works by artists from around the world. Second edition is still available. Write publisher for ordering details.

## UMBRELLA
P.O. Box 3692
Glendale, California 91201
Newsletter on current trends in art information and art views. Frequently contains information on rubber-stamp publications and events. Subscription is $12.50 per year.

## UNIVERSAL SHIP CANCELLATION SOCIETY LOG
417 Wilson Street
Sun Prairie, Wisconsin 53590

Monthly periodical devoted to ship cancellations. Subscription rate is $5 per year. Sometimes contains information on rubber-stamped cachets.

## U&lc
216 East 45th Street
New York, New York 10017
This fascinating journal, published quarterly, has run two articles about rubber stamps. The articles appeared in the September 1977 issue and the March 1978 issue. Back issues are available for $1.50 each. A one-year subscription is $6.

# RUBBER STAMP READING

Fischer, Herve.
**ART ET COMMUNICATION MARGINALE: TAMPONS d'ARTISTES.** Paris: Editions Andre Balland, 1974.

Friedman, Ken.
**A READY HAND NOVEL.** Skrakdhede, Ringkobing, Denmark: After Hand Editions, 1973.

Gaglione, Bill.
**THIS IS A SPECIAL RUBBER STAMP ART ISSUE OF DAD(D)AZINE.** San Francisco: Dadaland, 1976.

Kaprow, Allan.
**ASSEMBLAGES, ENVIRONMENT & HAPPENINGS.** New York: Harry N. Abrams, Inc., 1966.

Kocman, J.H.
**MONOGRAPHY OF MY STAMP ACTIVITY.** Brno, Czechoslovakia: Selbstverlag, 1974.

Kocman, J.H.
**STAMP ACTIVITY.** Brno, Czechoslovakia: Selbstverlag, 1972.

Mellone, Mike, and Planty, Dr. Earl.
**PLANTY'S PHOTO ENCYCLOPEDIA OF CACHETED FDCs.** New Jersey: F.D.C. Publishing Company.

Poinsot, Jean-Marc.
**MAIL ART: COMMUNICATION AT A DISTANCE, CONCEPT.** Paris: Editions C.E.D.I.C., 1971.

Rivard, Karen, and Brinkmann, Thomas H.
**THE MARKING STORY.** Illinois: Marking Device Association, 1968.

Rosenberg, Harold.
**SAUL STEINBERG.** New York: Alfred A. Knopf, Inc., 1978.

Roth, Dieter,
**MUNDUNCULUM.** Koln, Germany: Dumont, 1967.

Schmalenbach, Werner.
**KURT SCHWITTERS.** New York: Harry N. Abrams, Inc., 1967.

Sloane, T. O'Connor.
**RUBBER HAND STAMPS AND THE MANIPULATION OF RUBBER.** New York: Norman W. Henley & Co., 1891.

The End